simply slipcovers

Sunset

simply
slipcovers

BY THE EDITORS OF SUNSET BOOKS

SUNSET BOOKS INC. • MENLO PARK, CA

SUNSET BOOKS

VP, General Manager: Richard A. Smeby

VP, Editorial Director: Bob Doyle

Production Director: Lory Day

Art Director: Vasken Guiragossian

SIMPLY SLIPCOVERS was produced in conjunction with
Roundtable Press, Inc.

Directors: Marsha Melnick, Susan E. Meyer

STAFF FOR THIS BOOK:

Developmental Editor: Linda J. Selden

Senior Editor: Carol Spier

Book Design: Areta Buk/Thumb Print

Sample Coordinator and Technical Advisor: Linda Lee/Linda Lee Design Associates

Illustrations: Celia M. Mitchell

Photo Research: Ede Rothaus

Editorial Coordinators: Martha K. Moran, Caroline Politi

Technical Consultant: Zuelia Ann Hurt

Editorial Assistant: John Glenn

Production Coordinator: Patricia S. Williams

Cover Photograph: Philip Harvey; *Photo Direction:* JoAnn Masaoka Van Atta

Photography acknowledgments appear on page 128.

ISBN 0-376-01514-4

Library of Congress Catalog Card Number: 97-60899

Printed in the United States

For additional copies of SIMPLY SLIPCOVERS or any other *Sunset* book,
call 1-800-526-5111, or visit our website at
www.sunsetbooks.com

foreword

when you dress a chair or sofa in a slipcover, both the furniture and its setting take on a fresh character. Whatever your reason for changing your furniture's wardrobe—to alter its style, reflect the season, protect the upholstery, or disguise its color or condition—you'll find that making a slipcover is a two-part process—design decisions first, sewing second.

Simply Slipcovers is an inspirational and practical guide to slipcover making. It's filled with design ideas, includes twenty projects with step-by-step directions, and has a concise guide to the basic techniques you'll use.

Part One: Be Creative encourages you to put on your design cap and think creatively. It helps you analyze the way a slipcover will work in your decor, make design choices, and select materials. Photos of slipcovers in different styles and settings help you visualize the possibilities, while the text gives an overview of the design and construction process. This section will help you choose a slipcover you can make with confidence and use with pleasure.

Part Two: Projects features a selection of great-looking slipcovers and detailed illustrated directions for making them. The designs range from casual to formal, from tailored to sweet to sophisticated. Some projects are simple and can be quickly made even if you have little sewing experience, while others are quite complex.

As you look through the projects, you'll see that many include a special Designer Detail. These are construction and trimming techniques that add distinction; they're written generically so you can easily adapt them to other situations. You'll also see that each slipcover dresses a different type of furniture, so you can see how to fit and sew different shapes.

Part Three: Basics covers the general measuring, estimating, cutting, fitting, and sewing techniques you'll use to make any slipcover. It also identifies and explains the equipment you should have on hand.

Whether you'll be making one of the featured projects or designing your own slipcover, we encourage you to adapt the ideas and directions to suit your furniture and taste. Mix and match the slipcover silhouettes and the designer details; change color, fabric, and trim—be creative.

table of contents

part three
basics 96

designer details

be creative

SLIPCOVERS ARE TO FURNITURE WHAT CLOTHING IS to the body. They camouflage, dress up or down, give character, and convey style. They also protect upholstery. Like clothing, they can be utilitarian or festive, traditional or unique—and changed at whim. While slipcovers can mimic the upholstery they mask, they also offer a great way to transform your decor from formal to casual, traditional to exotic. They can add color, pattern, softness, or wit; give a seasonal lift; and make an odd piece of furniture feel at home. Unlike clothing, most slipcovers must be designed and made to order, and with few exceptions, commercial patterns are not available.

thinking creatively

you are no doubt asking yourself where to begin. As with any decorating project, begin with creativity. Whether you intend to make your own slipcovers, employ an interior designer, or work directly with a sewing contractor, you'll need a clear idea of what you want. And to be sure your slipcover is everything you desire, you need to know more than what you want it to look like—you need to define its purpose and place within your decor. Moreover, if you're planning to do the work yourself, you'll want to be sure you have the necessary skills and equipment. So start by answering some questions.

Are you decorating or redecorating? Creating a whole new ambience, or just changing one or two pieces? Will you be integrating your slipcover with a new or existing decor?

When furniture is lightly padded or not upholstered at all, the subtle quiltlike texture of matelassé gives an inviting sense of softness and volume. Here a simple, fringe-trimmed slipcover skims the clean lines of a sculptural chair.

What is the purpose of your slipcover? To dress your decor up or down or otherwise change the ambience? To protect upholstery? To mask furniture that doesn't go with the rest of your decor? To provide a seasonal change or be always in use? Are you looking for a quick or temporary fix or a lasting solution?

What about style and ambience? What style is the furniture you plan to cover? Do you want to cover it in a traditional or unconventional manner? What kind and how much of a statement should your slipcover make? Quiet? Breathtaking? Casual? Witty? Tailored? Have you considered the trims and details of a potential design as well as its overall silhouette?

Are you making the slipcover yourself? What sort of skills do you have? Do you understand what the straight grain of the fabric is? Do you consider your sewing machine a friend or foe? Is it sturdy enough for the task in mind? Do you have a good steam iron? Do you have enough space to lay out your fabric,

and manipulate the large pieces while you are assembling them—or to store your project while in process? How complex a project are you contemplating?

How much money are you willing to spend? Slipcovers tend to be costly. Even if you do the work yourself, you're likely to need quite a bit of fabric and will invest a fair amount of time. If you'd really rather have new upholstery, find out what the cost would be—it might not be much more.

As you ask these questions, you'll see that the answers work together to help you decide what sort of slipcover you want and need. But consider also that no matter how inspired you are, or how clear your design vision, each piece of furniture is unique, with its own requirements and challenges. While slipcovers are more cumbersome than difficult to sew, making one for *your* piece of furniture will inevitably present a puzzle that will require ingenuity to solve.

This book offers many design ideas and features twenty projects with directions. If you like the projects and your furniture is similar to ours, you may be able to follow the instructions as written or with minor adaptations. You may want to mix and match the details we show to make your own designs. Of course, there is no reason to stop with our ideas; after all, we don't know your taste or needs. So be creative, design your own slipcovers, and incorporate any ideas or concepts you find here or elsewhere. To get off to a confident start, read Basics, pages 97–126—you'll find the general measuring information critical. And do take the time to plan ahead—it's the professional way to start.

Less can certainly be more, as demonstrated by the tailored slipcovers enhancing this contemporary room. Their design could not be less complicated. Contrasting neutrals on the sofa relieve what could be a boring expanse. Large club chairs look equally sophisticated in striped or plain fabric.

slipcover design

Graceful English country patterns are both elegant and fresh. Mix florals, stripes, and floral stripes; contrast with a crisp gingham check or a trompe l'oeil drapery print for fun. Keep the palette consistent and the scale varied.

The covers in this formal room are fresh yet properly dressy, with grand fringe and bicolor cording on the sofa, contrasting welting outlining the armchairs. Note the coordinating floral stripe used for the chair skirts.

when you contemplate the design possibilities for your slipcover, think of several interdependent things. Think first of the furniture—its shape and size and its place in your decor. Think of the style you want for the slipcover. And think about possible fabrics and the way in which their color, pattern, texture, sheen, weight, and opacity will interact with the rest of your decor. The object of the design process is to devise a slipcover that sits stylishly in its surroundings. Part of this process is creative, part is practical— you want to design something that you can make.

Begin your design process by collecting ideas. Clip pictures from magazines and catalogs, visit furniture stores and designer show houses if you can. Identify why the ideas are appealing to you. Is it the shape, the color, the fabric, the trim details? Is it the proportions, perhaps a daring hemline, or the way in which the cover fits? Or is it something unconventional or especially clever about the overall design? Do you understand how the effect was achieved? Whatever it is, is it something you can closely copy or will you have to make considerable adjustments to adapt it to your furniture?

slipcover design

Humble slipcovers don't mask the elegance of these formal chairs, they just impart a temporarily casual air. The long wrapped ties remind us that style lies in the details.

As you design, bear in mind that the most difficult slipcovers to make are those that simulate upholstery. The tighter the cover, the more accurate your cutting, fitting, and sewing have to be. Unless you are very confident of your pattern-making and sewing skills, you will probably be happiest with a project that is loose fitting or informal, casual or in some way eclectic. As you look through decorating magazines, you'll see that informal designs are by no means unsophisticated—with the right fabrication they work in almost any decor. You should feel free to do the unexpected. Covers can have several layers, they can be controlled and secured with ties. Most importantly, fabric color and pattern can be used creatively—you can mix complementary patterns or cut some parts of the cover from contrasting colors.

The fun of design lies in selecting which details to incorporate. Unless a slipcover is simply a large unconstructed sheet of fabric draped and tied over the furniture, it is likely to include a shaped "envelope" for each principal component—the back, seat, and arms. Your challenge is to embellish the envelopes so as to give your design a unique character. Embellishments might include matching or contrasting welting in the seams; flat, pleated, or gathered skirts to cover the legs; decorative closures, such as bows or ties; and applied trims, such as fringe and tassels. The way in which you use these—their color, material, proportion—or your choice to omit them altogether, will give your design panache. Remember that in slipcover design, as in clothing, less is often more, and simple embellishments can be very effective. Consider edging a hem with a contrasting band of ribbon, or trimming a striped cover with bias-cut ruffles or welting, or concentrating skirt fullness at corners rather than distributing it evenly around the chair.

If you need help visualizing your ideas on your furniture, do a little experimenting early on. Start by pinning twill tape or string on your furniture (use drafting tape on wood or metal surfaces) to mark potential seamlines and refer to these when measuring. If you are making one of the designs for which we give directions, make an inexpensive muslin mock-up to check the fit and proportions: Cut the pieces with generous seam allowances, and adjust them until the muslin fits the way you wish. If you are designing your own cover, drape a mock-up right over your chair or sofa. You can make the mock-up as loose or as tight as you wish your slipcover to be; pin, tape, or draw seams where you think they should go; and use pins to arrange folds, gathers, or pleats as needed. This is a sure way to judge proportions and see right away if your idea is feasible. If you mark the seamlines on the muslin before you disassemble it, it can serve as a pattern. You can even trace your fabric pattern onto the muslin to work out the match points. Expect to work intuitively; each slipcover is unique and your instincts will be your best guide.

Before you finalize your design, look at samples of the fabric and trims in the room where the furniture sits. You'll want to be sure that the colors, patterns, textures, and weights look well with your other furnishings. (If you are undertaking a major decorating or redecorating task and feel insecure about creating color schemes, you'll find many good books on the subject in the decorating and art sections of bookstores and libraries.) Look at samples in natural and artificial light. Drape them over your furniture to get an idea of the way the fabric will fall when made up. Crush fabrics to see if they wrinkle badly, crease them to see if they will hold a pleat. If you can't borrow a sample from a supplier, don't economize by skipping this step— buy a piece large enough to show how the fabric works.

Textured linen is at home in many settings. Here, a casually cut slipcover combines with big throw pillows to mask a formal loveseat, bringing a contemporary country touch to a period home.

choosing fabric

The muted tones of faded floral prints are comfortable, relaxing, and vaguely antique. Choose a primary pattern, accent with smaller patterns in the same tones, use other large patterns elsewhere in the room.

A loosely fitted slipcover on a big squishy piece of furniture invites relaxation. The gathered skirt adds an unexpected frill to the spare lines of this open room; white cotton saves the effect from fussiness.

slipcovers are made of fabric, and fabric offers you a world of design possibilities. You may know from the outset what type of fabric you wish to use—you may even know the specific pattern. But if you do not, bear in mind that while there are times when a design concept begs to be interpreted in a specific fabric, there are other times when a fabric will suggest a design concept. Be open to both possibilities.

When you are designing, it is important to think about the aesthetic as well as the practical characteristics of fabric. Fabric allows you to introduce color, pattern, and texture to your decor. *Pattern* may relate to or establish a style. When you think of styles such as country, lodge, French or English, Victorian or another period, distinct pattern images come to mind for each.

Color establishes mood and can change your perception of space or proportion—and some palettes are associated with specific decorating styles. *Texture* contributes to the way a fabric reflects or absorbs light, and thus affects its color. Fabrics can be smooth, soft, crisp, or coarse textured—or a combination of these. Fabrics such as bouclé, velvet, and corduroy have texture that adds dimension. The structure of a fabric's weave, the type and weight of the fiber it is made from, and the finish it is given all contribute to its texture. These last characteristics also give each kind of fabric its *hand*— a term used to describe the way a fabric handles, or behaves, indicating how stable it is, how well it drapes, how bulky it is—and they make it suitable to use for certain effects. Additionally, while slipcover fabrics are usually opaque, sheer and translucent textiles can be used with great effect.

Country prints seasoned with French charm are easy to mix. You can start with coordinated fabrics or put together your own assortment—balance large and small florals with geometrics and scenics—but control yourself; don't use them all.

Confused? Even though you may not be familiar with the jargon applied to fabrics, you should use your eyes and hands to get an idea of a fabric's suitability. Crisp fabrics do not usually drape or mold well. Depending upon the desired effect, they may or may not make good ruffles. Thick fabrics can be bulky and unattractive when gathered or pleated or made up as welting. Soft or slippery fabrics may be difficult to control, and may not wear well. Sheers reveal the lines, colors, and defects of the furniture they cover; they can be effective or inappropriate as slipcovers. Visit furniture stores to get a firsthand look at the way different fabrics are used, and be sure to handle a good-sized sample of any fabric you contemplate using before you purchase it. Just as it is always a good idea to borrow or buy sample yardage to see its effect in your room, it is also a good idea to make a few test seams to be sure you like the way it handles.

choosing fabric

To enliven a tailored decor, mix solid fabrics with contemporary graphic patterns. Here the related hues of a funky tapestry, a "conversation print," and a geometric complement plain velvet and linen.

What kind of fabric should you use? For durable slipcovers, home furnishings fabrics—often called decorator fabrics—are best. They not only offer great aesthetic options, they've been engineered to have a suitable hand, wear well, and are often stain resistant. Additionally, they're usually quite wide (54"–60") so they're more efficient to work with. Depending upon where you live, a wide selection of decorator fabrics may be available at local fabric stores. If not, you can often order them through a furnishings store or interior designer.

Home furnishings fabrics can be very costly, and slipcovers require a surprising amount of yardage. If you don't view your slipcover (or its chair) as a long-term player in your decor, if your budget is limited, or you're just looking for a quick source of wide fabrics, consider using tablecloths or bedspreads (which often have great border and corner motifs), or sheets. For a quick, no-sew cover, you can even drape your sofa with a humble painter's drop cloth (unbleached cotton twill already pieced and available at hardware stores). Some apparel fabrics can be used, but they are not always as durable, and if narrower, any savings may be offset by the greater yardage requirements.

When you are considering fabrics, don't confuse fiber with fabric. Fiber is what fabric is made of. Fibers are either natural—cotton, linen, silk, wool— or man-made. Some man-made fibers are created from natural materials; rayon, for example, is derived from wood. Others, such as nylon, polyester, and acrylic, are true synthetics; these are often petroleum-based. The way a fiber is spun, woven, and finished determines the kind of fabric it becomes. There are many, many kinds of fabric (broadcloth, velveteen, chintz, damask— to name just a few), and many, but not all, can be made from more than one fiber.

Slipcover fabrics are most often made of cotton, which is durable; comes in many weaves, weights, and finishes; and can be washed. It is also easy to handle. Because it is not slippery, cotton is likely to sit tidily on your furniture. Linen is another popular choice; it wears like iron but beware its famous wrinkles. Decorator fabrics are often blends of cotton and other fibers, usually linen or rayon, but sometimes silk or wool or a synthetic, such as polyester. Elegant fabrics sometimes feature metallic threads as well. Linen, rayon, and silk all add sheen and take dye well, so fabrics made with them often appear luxurious and have especially intense colors. Like cotton, silk comes in many weights, textures, and finishes, and the different silks have widely varying characteristics—ranging from fragile to durable, easy to handle to frustratingly slippery. Some silks are washable, but many of those water-spot easily and a single drop of condensation from a cold

glass can make them look soiled. Most silks are extremely sensitive to sunlight, fade badly, and sometimes deteriorate with constant exposure. One hundred percent rayon is difficult to handle and not particularly durable. The more synthetic content a fabric has, the less well it will take a crease, and the better it will hold a stain. On the whole, it is best to avoid fabrics with a high synthetic content, but textile engineers are constantly improving them, so if one appeals, ask a reputable vendor about it.

If you're looking for a dressy yet unpretentious look, mix velvet with a relaxed design. Here it gives understated elegance to a classic loosely cut sofa cover. You'll find velvet and its relative chenille in many wonderful colors and subtle textures.

choosing fabric

Summery checks are always welcome in a country decor. The semibold scale of bistro gingham is a perfect choice for the chaise in this room, balancing nimbly between the wall covering and quilt. Note the ruffles inserted in the cushion edges.

What about weave and finish? Slipcover fabrics should have a fairly tight weave; they should feel stable, but not stiff, when you handle them. Medium-weight, nonpile, nonslippery fabrics are the easiest to work with. The most commonly chosen fabrics are those with plain, twill, or damask (single-color motif-patterned) weaves; satin weaves are sometimes used as well, especially to create stripes. Jacquard or tapestry weaves are more difficult to work with, as they are bulky and fray easily. Printed fabrics usually, but not always, have a plain or twill weave. Plain and twill weaves sometimes have a glazed finish, cotton chintz being an example. Some home furnishings fabrics are treated with a stain repellent, and while the fabric may be washable, the repellent might not be, so ask your vendor before preshrinking or laundering these.

Which fabric will be suitable? It depends on the effect you want to achieve. This is why it is so important to test the *hand*—the feel and drape—of your fabric, and not to base your selection on color and pattern alone. Consider also the furniture you are covering and the amount of use it gets. And if you will be making the slipcover yourself, be sure your sewing machine can sew through at least six layers of the fabric without complaint.

What kind of fabric patterns are best? "The kinds you like" is the first answer to this question, but bear in mind that your skill as a pattern maker, cutter, and sewer are more critical when you work with patterns that need careful matching. If you are covering upholstered furniture or any piece with curving seams, stay away from plaids and checks and be cautious about stripes. Patterns with obvious repeats or dominant motifs require careful matching; they're more difficult to lay out and sew, and you'll probably need much more fabric, so they can be costly to use. On the other hand, good use of a fabric pattern can really enhance your slipcover design. Use plaids and checks for contrasting ruffles or welting, turn stripes forty-five or ninety degrees to band a hem or box a cushion. Many manufacturers offer coordinated prints in their fabric lines, which makes it easy for you to mix and match as you wish.

What about fabric quality? Be a savvy consumer. Purchase your fabric from a reputable vendor. Be sure the fiber content and maintenance requirements are clearly identified. Buy all of each color or pattern from one bolt because dye lots can vary. If using a print, make sure it falls squarely on grain (perpendicular and parallel to the woven edge, called the selvage). When you go to match an off-square pattern you'll have to sacrifice either the grainline (which will spoil the way your cover hangs) or the pattern alignment. Sometimes the grain of handwoven fabrics and lightweight silks is not perfectly square, which, depending upon your intended fabrication, may be problematic.

What about cost? Slipcovers are an investment. Most of them take quite a bit of fabric, and you're likely to spend a fair amount of time making one. So don't take the cost lightly—if you are going to spend the time and want the cover to wear well, it will be worthwhile to use the best fabric you can afford.

Dining chair slipcovers turn their backs to a room without offense, presenting a wonderful chance to mix fabrics. Here a formal print front sports a tattersall back.

choosing trim

welting, cords, buttons, tassels, frogs, lace, ribbon, even sporty rickrack—trims lend polish and panache to slipcovers. Visually, trims should be in scale with and have the same weight as the slipcover. You will probably find the best selection in a home furnishings fabric store. Trims meant for apparel are often too small and too flimsy to look or wear well on slipcovers.

If you like trims, you're likely to find shopping for them both exhilarating and frustrating. There are so many choices, you'll no doubt be inspired to take advantage of them. But select wisely; you may be surprised by their cost. If trim is an important part of your slipcover's design, be sure you can find what you want before you purchase the fabric; you may want to rethink one or the other till you find a mix that looks great and fits your budget.

Most decorator trims are made of cotton or rayon or a blend of the two. They come in myriad colors, yet finding a perfect match for your fabric may prove virtually impossible. But a trim that makes a subtle or strong contrast can be more interesting than one that blends into its background—that's why you use trim anyway. When you want a perfect match, welting, cording, or binding made from your fabric may be the most appropriate choice. Some vendors can arrange to have trims such as tassels made to order, and many good notions retailers have a button-covering service. If you plan to wash your slipcover, be sure the trim is washable, and preshrink it before using. Rayon trim is especially likely to shrink.

Don't be shy when choosing trims—fringe, cording, braid, and tassels should be in proportion to the furniture and the fabric pattern. Here a striking print is enhanced by a multicolored fringe set into the seams and topstitched to the hem.

A few embellishment options offer myriad effects. Here are three fabrics and three trims in fourteen combinations. Mix florals and geometrics; use matching or contrasting welting, binding, or even a hem band; add fringe or gimp over or under a seam or hem.

into the workroom

be creative, be focused, be confident—let these phrases guide you through your slipcover making. If you gather ideas and analyze your needs, and then take the time to plan your project, you should be able to follow through with flair.

If you are an inexperienced sewer, or haven't sewn in a while, choose a simple project for your first slipcover. On the other hand, if you're experienced and confident, you should be able to make any of the projects in this book, or any other slipcover you can visualize and analyze. Whatever your experience, do take the time to read all the directions before you begin, and think through the steps involved to be sure you understand them. Professional designers and sewing contractors will be the first to tell you that the work they do before scissors meet fabric—the designing, fabric selection, measuring, and pattern making—can easily take as much time as the actual sewing. By spending this time, they assure that the sewing goes smoothly and yields terrific results.

Texture can be as important to the look of a slipcover as color or pattern. These fabrics share a neutral palette, but coarse and fine threads; damask, velvet, plain, and twill weaves, and even quilting, create varied effects—and handle differently.

A blue and white ticking slipcover skims the wing chair at right, the stripes beautifully matched at each horizontal seam. The red and white slipcover is finished discreetly by a self-bias welting at the lower edge; ties under the chair keep it tidy.

projects

VIRTUALLY ANY CHAIR, BENCH, OR SOFA CAN BE
enhanced with a slipcover. Following are twenty
designs—fun, formal, casual, elegant—with
directions. You can make them as shown or adapt
them as suits your needs or fancy. Check out the
Designer Detail features—these explain special
sewing and trimming techniques you can use as
we have, or apply to other projects. Throughout
the directions you'll find Tips from the Pros—hints
and tricks to smooth your work. So browse through
the photos to pick a design, read the step-by-step
directions, refer to the watercolor illustrations, and
get started.

how to use the directions

Each project in this book can be made by following its illustrated step-by-step directions. To understand the components of these directions, read these two pages. Because each piece of furniture is different, you may have to adapt the directions so the design works for your chair or sofa.

1 A colored fabric panel begins each project. It contains information you need before you begin to sew.

2 MATERIALS

Here you will find a description of the fabric(s) used to make the sample in the photograph, including any lining. You will also find listed other necessary materials, such as trims, thread, and other notions.

✄The fabric width and yardage used give you an idea of the fabric required for a similar project. Take time to calculate your specific fabric needs.

✄To calculate the amount of trim you need, you must measure the slipcover edges and seams that will be trimmed; refer to the cutting directions further down in this panel, the step-by-step directions, and the photos.

3 TECHNIQUES

This paragaph refers you to Part Three of the book, Basics. There you will find information to help you measure, calculate yardage, fit your cover, and sew it together. Review this section, as it supports and enhances the project directions. Use the index at the end of the book to locate specific information.

4 MEASURE, MARK, AND CUT

The note that begins this section alerts you to aspects of the project that may not be apparent from the photo, such as when to allow extra fabric for pleats or facings, where to use a lining or padding, or where to place a seam. For instance, the note in this example tells you how to allow for the thickness of the chair back, where to add a facing, and also gives the number of pleats in the skirt.

5 CUTTING LIST

This names each piece needed to make the slipcover, including facings and bias strips for welting or binding, and tells you how many of each to cut.

✄The letter identifying each piece is repeated in the measuring diagram, cutting layout, and directions.

6 MEASURING DIAGRAM(S)

Each project is accompanied by one or two simplified drawings of the furniture. These diagrams show where to measure your furniture to determine the size of each piece of the slipcover. The measuring diagrams usually, but not always, appear in the colored fabric panel.

✂ The arrows indicate which dimensions to measure. The solid outlines indicate slipcover seams that fall over the upholstery seams or on logical edges of the furniture. The dash lines indicate seams that have been added to create the slipcover design, for instance the line at which to attach or hem a skirt.

✂ The letter on each section identifies the piece as given in the cutting list.

Measure each section at its longest and widest point; include the thickness of the furniture if appropriate. If a piece wraps around the furniture, the arrow curves to indicate this and the arrowheads meet on the back view of the furniture.

✂ Refer to Part Three to see how to record these measurements and add seam, hem, tuck-in, and pin-fitting allowances to them. Once you have added the allowances, you will have the cutting dimensions for each piece.

✂ Remember that the final shape and proportion of most slipcovers will be determined by fitting the cut-out pieces on the furniture.

7 CUTTING LAYOUT(S)

A suggested cutting layout is given for each fabric. The layouts show the fabric spread flat in a single layer. The cutting layouts are always on the first page of the directions; their exact position varies.

✂ The outline of each piece is drawn on the layout and the piece is identified by letter. When two or more of a piece are needed, each is drawn and labeled—except for bias strips and ties, which are labeled only once.

✂ Portions of the layout that are not labeled indicate excess fabric.

✂ Refer to Part Three to see how to make a layout. Depending upon your furniture and fabric, your layout may be very different from the one illustrated. For instance, if you were not trying to take advantage of a dominant pattern, you might be able to cut the skirt for this slipcover on the crosswise grain.

8 STEP-BY-STEP DIRECTIONS

To make it easy to keep your place, each step of the directions is numbered. Review the information in the colored fabric panel, cut out your slipcover pieces, and then follow the directions in the sequence given. Read the directions through before beginning to be sure you understand the nature of the project.

✂ The first time a piece is handled, it is identified by letter as well as by name.

✂ If a step is illustrated, an arrow at the end of the step points to the pertinent illustration. The illustration can be above, below, or next to the text.

✂ If a technique or process is more fully explained in Part Three, this information is cross-referenced within the numbered steps.

9 TIPS FROM THE PROS

Throughout the project directions, we've included hints, tips, and words of wisdom to smooth your work. These usually follow the step to which they pertain, so read the step and the subsequent tips before proceeding.

10 DESIGNER DETAIL

It's the finishing touches that give real polish to a slipcover design, and many of the projects in this book are enhanced by special "designer details." Each has been placed under a colored fabric flag and explained with extra attention to ensure that you'll be able to sew it successfully.

✂ The use of these details is by no means limited to the ways in which we've featured them. The flags make it easy for you to see the details separately from the projects, and we encourage you to think of other ways to use them—so be creative.

TWO IMPORTANT NOTES

✂ The standard seam allowance for slipcover making is $1/2$".

✂ Any measurements given in the measuring note, cutting list, or step-by-step directions reflect those used to make the sample in the photo. Check and adjust the proportions to suit your fabric or furniture.

futon sham

MATERIALS

*Fabric: Shown in print denim, this model
required 3 yards of 54"-wide fabric.
Buttons
Ribbon
Thread to match*

TECHNIQUES

*Refer to Part Three for information on
calculating yardage and basic sewing
techniques.*

MEASURE, MARK, AND CUT

*Note: Futon cover should not fit tightly.
Refer to the schematic drawing as you
calculate the dimensions. Measure the
lengthwise distance around the futon
and add four times the desired flange
depth plus 6" for hems. Measure and
add together the width and thickness of
the futon, add two times the desired
flange depth, divide the total for panels,
and add seam allowance.*

(A) **SIDE PANELS**

(B) **CENTRAL PANEL**

1 Sew a side
panel (A) to each
side of the center
panel (B). ▽

TIPS FROM THE PROS

✂Futons are heavy and cumbersome.
Reinforce the seams of your
slipcover so they'll survive intact
when you dress and undress the futon
(refer to Basics, page 115, for
flat-felled and other sturdy seam
instructions).

2 Hem the ends for the envelope
closure: At each end fold 2" of
fabric to the wrong side and press;
fold 2" again and press. Topstitch
along inner folded edge. Determine
the number of buttonholes needed
and, placing them at least 10"
from the sides, mark within the
hem on one end.
Stitch buttonholes
at the marks. ▽

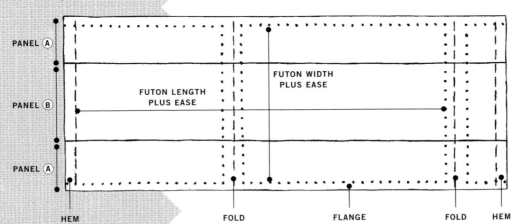

PANEL (A)		FUTON WIDTH PLUS EASE	FLANGE DEPTH SHOWN IS 3 1/2"
PANEL (B)	FUTON LENGTH PLUS EASE		ADD SEAM ALLOWANCE ON BOTH LONG EDGES OF
PANEL (A)			EACH PANEL

HEM   FOLD   FLANGE   FOLD   HEM

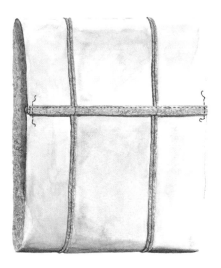

This informal futon cover is like a giant pillow sham.

3 Place the fabric right side up. Fold the buttonhole end up. Fold the other end up and lap it over the buttonhole end. Pin the overlapped hems together at their ends and baste. ◁

4 With the right side still inside, shift the overlap so it lies across the fabric about one-quarter of the way from one folded end. Pin and sew the side edges together, stitching over the basting at the hem ends. Turn the slipcover right side out through the overlapped hems. Press the seams and each folded end to crease sharply.

5 Mark a line 3¹/₂" from the outer edges. Baste along the marked line through all layers. ▽

easy futon sham

6 Referring to the Designer Detail below, couch decorative ribbon over the basting line.

7 Mark the button placement on the hem without buttonholes and sew on the buttons.

Bright red buttons jazz up the back closure, (left). Matching ribbon covers the topstitching that secures the flange (below).

designer detail
couched trim

Couching is a method of securing narrow trim to a surface with stitches that pass over rather than through the trim itself. When the stitches are the correct size, couched trims lie flat without puckering. They can usually be sewn on without preliminary basting or pinning. Soutache and other flexible trims will follow curved lines well. The stitches can match or contrast the trim. To begin, mark the pattern you wish the trim to cover onto the right side of your fabric.

1 Set your machine to a long zigzag stitch that is slightly wider than the trim. Choose an appropriate starting place on the marked pattern, and place that portion of the project in the machine, right side up.

TIPS FROM THE PROS
✂Always test your couching technique on a swatch—use the same layers of fabric and interfacing as are in your project.
✂Use a fabric glue stick to hold the trim in place when mitering corners or following other tricky shapes.

2 Lay narrow trim on top of the marked pattern line, with the end of the trim behind the needle. Zigzag stitch over the trim, turning the project and feeding more trim under the presser foot as needed.
✂Miter trim corners neatly.
✂Join trim ends by overlapping or butting as appropriate; use a shorter zigzag stitch to secure.

smart adjustable slipcover

1 Referring to the Designer Detail on page 35, bind both bottom edges of the front/back (A), the bottom edge of each arm (B), and the bottom edge of each gusset (C) and (D); the ends of the binding will be covered later.

2 With the fabric right side out, lay the front/back over the chair. Align the bound edges with the floor in front and back and tuck in the excess behind the cushion.

3 With the fabric right side out, lay each arm over the chair. Align the bound edge with the floor on the side and rest the opposite end on the seat cushion.

4 With the fabric right side out and the bound edge aligned with the floor, pin each side gusset in place. Begin pinning at the floor on the back edge, work up over the top curve, and stop at the top of the arm. Pin the remaining edge to the arm, begin pinning at the floor, and stop at the top of the arm. ◁

This cover is sewn together right side out. Bias binding encloses the seams, side and front gussets add dimension, and bows control the fit.

MATERIALS
Fabric: Shown in striped cotton, this model required 7 yards of 56"-wide fabric.
Thread to match

TECHNIQUES
Refer to Part Three for information on measuring, calculating yardage, pin fitting, and basic sewing techniques.

MEASURE, MARK, AND CUT
Note: Make a pattern for each gusset, or cut as rectangles and refine when pin fitting. Add 1" seam allowances on all but the bottom edge of each piece; no hem allowance is necessary.

(A) **FRONT/BACK** ✂ add tuck-in to length
(B) **ARM** ✂ cut 2, add tuck-in to length
(C) **FRONT GUSSET** ✂ cut 2
(D) **SIDE GUSSET** ✂ cut 2
(E) **TIES** ✂ cut 12, 7" x 28" each
(F) **BIAS STRIPS** ✂ cut 4" wide, to go around the bottom of chair and the sides and top of each gusset

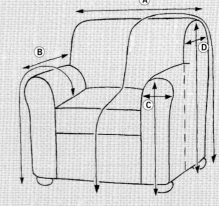

smart adjustable slipcover

5 In the same manner, pin each front gusset in place. Begin pinning at the floor on the side edge, work up over the top curve, and stop at the top of the cushion. Pin the remaining edge to the front, begin pinning at the floor, and stop at the bottom of the cushion. Fold the excess arm fabric to make the tuck-in on each side of the cushion, but leave unpinned for now. ▽

6 Pin the remaining edges of each arm to the adjacent edge of the front/back. Begin pinning at the top front edge of the cushion, work to the back edge, then pull out the tuck-in allowance behind the cushion. Begin pinning again at the top of the arm, work down the inside of the arm, pleating in any excess arm fabric as needed.

To use this design on a nonupholstered armchair (such as a director's chair), just make the gussets narrower.

7 Remove the slipcover from the chair and sew all the seams as pinned, leaving the seam allowance on the outside: First sew the seams pinned in step 6; finish the cut edges. Then refold and sandwich each tuck-in between the adjacent front and side gusset edges; pin. Sew all the remaining seams.

8 Make twelve 3"-wide ties, leaving one end of each unfinished (refer to Basics, page 121).

9 Place the slipcover on the chair; tuck in the excess at the back and sides of the cushion (vertical tucks will form to conceal the arm/back seams). Matching cut edges, pin one pair of ties to each front gusset and two pairs to each side gusset where appropriate. Tie into bows to check length and position. ▷

10 Untie the bows and remove the cover from the chair. Referring to the Designer Detail, opposite, bind the remaining seam allowances; remember to finish the ends of all the binding strips at the bottom edge of the slipcover.

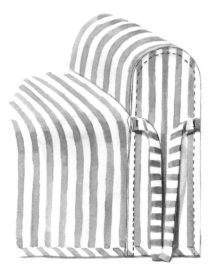

decorative bias binding

When you are looking for a way to finish cut edges that is both decorative and functional, consider enclosing them in bias binding. The adjustable slipcover is sewn with all the seams on the outside, and we used this technique to finish its bottom edges and seam allowances.

1 Determine the finished width of the binding (1" here) then multiply this dimension by 4 to find the width to cut the bias strips. Cut the bias strips. Join them as necessary (refer to Basics, page 117).

For a different effect, use a solid-color fabric for the binding. Or make the cover from one solid, the binding from another.

2 With wrong side in, fold the bias strip in half lengthwise, aligning the cut edges. Press. Unfold the strip; align each cut edge with the crease. Press. ▽

3 Unfold one edge of the bias binding. With the right sides together and cut edges aligned, pin the binding to the edge of the project.

✂ If you are enclosing seam allowance, the crease nearest the binding edge should align with the seamline.

✂ If the end of the binding will be covered (as on the bottom edges of this cover) it should align with the adjacent (vertical) edge of the piece.

✂ If the end of the binding will be finished (as at the bottom of a gusset seam) it should extend ¹/₂" beyond the end of the seam.

✂ Sew the binding in place along the crease. ▽

4 Press the seam allowance toward the binding, the binding away from the project.

✂ Fold any extending bias strip ends over the seam ends to cover them.

5 Fold the binding over the cut edge of the seam allowance, covering both sides of the seam allowance and aligning the folded edge of the binding with the seamline. Pin. ▽

6 Fold the entire binding toward the right side of the project. Zigzag stitch along the folded edge, letting alternate stitches catch the edge of the binding and the project. ▽

TIPS FROM THE PROS
✂ Use monofilament thread for an invisible zigzag stitch.
✂ Don't try to place a wide binding over a narrow seam allowance.

folding chair cover

MATERIALS

Fabric: Shown in lightweight cotton canvas, this model required 2 yards of 54"-wide fabric, plus 1/2 yard of contrasting fabric for the hem band.
Decorative piping (with a flange)
Buttons
Thread to match

TECHNIQUES

Refer to Part Three for information on measuring, calculating yardage, pin fitting, and basic sewing techniques.

MEASURE, MARK, AND CUT

Note: Determine the seat band width by measuring around the chair at seat level and at the dash line on the drawing; use the larger number. Determine the minimum skirt width by measuring loosely around the chair legs at the floorline; the skirt and hem band should each be 32" bigger than the seat band to include four pairs of 2"-deep pleats. Cut the hem band to twice the finished depth plus seam allowance.

Ⓐ INSIDE BACK
Ⓑ OUTSIDE BACK
Ⓒ SEAT
Ⓓ SEAT BAND
✂cut as many panels as needed
Ⓔ HEM BAND
✂cut as many panels as needed
Ⓕ SKIRT ✂cut as many panels as needed

1 Pin-fit the inside back (A) and outside back (B) on the chair, forming two dartlike tucks on the bottom edge of the inside back. Pin-fit the seat (C) to the inside back. Mark the outer edge of the seat, continuing the line around the bottom edge of the back. ▽

2 Remove the pinned pieces from the chair, true up the seamlines, disassemble the pieces, and mark the seam allowances. Trim the excess fabric. Baste the tucks in place. Sew piping to the right side of the inside back along the sides and across the top (refer to Basics pages 119 and 117). △

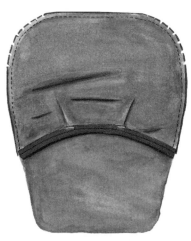

3 Sew the seat to the inside back, stopping the stitches at the outer seamlines. Then sew the inside back and outside back together along the top and sides. △

4 Sew piping to the right side of the lower edge of the assembled seat/back, joining the ends appropriately (refer to Basics page 119). ▽

5 Sew the ends of the seat band (D) together to make a ring; press the seam open. Pin and sew the seat band to the piped edge of the seat/back. Sew piping to the right side of the lower edge of the seat band. ▽

6 Referring to the Designer Detail on page 38, sew a hem band (E) to the bottom of each skirt panel (F).

A contrasting hem and decorative buttons lend a prim and proper air to a conventional folding chair. Of course, you can adapt this design to fit a regular side chair.

7 Before sewing the skirt panels together, place the cover on the chair and pin-fit them, right side out, to the seat, folding a 2"-deep inverted pleat on each side of each corner; place any seams on the inverted fold of a pleat. Mark the pleats and the corresponding corners of the band. ▷

TIPS FROM THE PROS
✄Be sure the skirt fits loosely over the chair legs at the floor; adjust if necessary.

snappy cover

8 Sew the skirt panels together, stitching through all layers of the hem band at once so the pleat will fold crisply on the seam, then finish the seam allowance. Repin the pleats as marked (do not open the skirt panel seam) and baste across the top edge.

9 Pin and sew the skirt to the lower edge of the band.

10 Trim the skirt by sewing decorative buttons, evenly spaced, just below the seat band.

Buttons parade all the way around, making the back view every bit as appealing as the front.

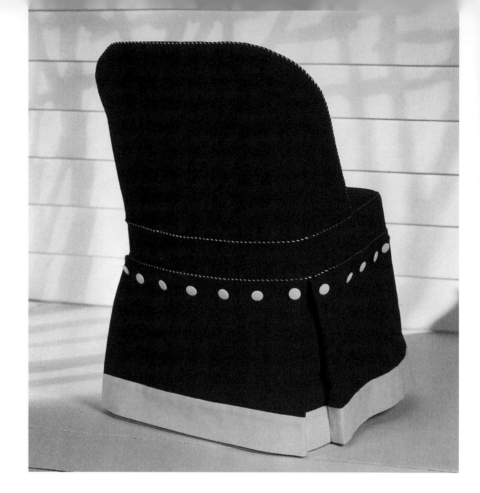

designer detail

contrasting borders

It is easy to dress up a slipcover skirt with a contrasting self-faced border. Cut the border to twice the desired finished depth, plus seam allowance. Also be sure to allow seam allowance on the bottom of the skirt.

TIPS FROM THE PROS

✂ To enable a pleated skirt to fold crisply on a seam, sew on the border as described here and then join the ends of the skirt, sewing through all layers at once. For a nonpleated skirt like the one on page 66, join the ends of the skirt after step 2 and press the seam allowance open. When you refold the border in step 3, the vertical seam will be covered by the inside of the border.

1 With wrong sides together, press the band in half lengthwise. Open it out. Finish one long edge of the band.

2 With right sides together, sew the unfinished edge of the band to the bottom of the skirt. ▽

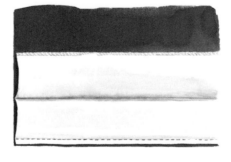

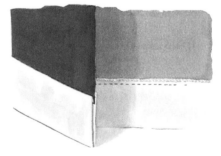

3 Press the seam allowance toward the band. Refold the band to the wrong side along the creaseline. Pin the finished edge over the seam allowance. On the right side, stitch in the ditch of the seamline, sewing through the underside of the band. △

welted cover-up

1 Lay the inside back/seat (A) on the chair; pin to it the front skirt (B) and the two outside back/side skirts (C). Pin the side front seams, stopping 8$^1/_2$" from the lower edges; also pin the center back seam, stopping 4$^1/_2$" from the top edge. Mark the seamlines and match points; also mark the seat height on the center back slit edges. Trim the excess seam allowance. ▽

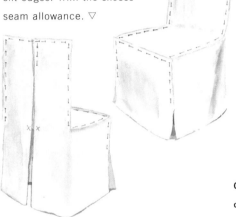

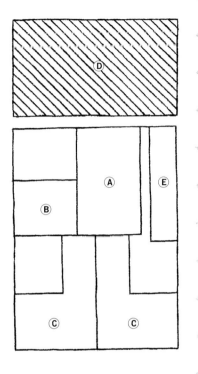

Contrasting welting adds spice to the edges of an otherwise uncomplicated slipcover.

MATERIALS

Fabric: Shown in lightweight cotton canvas, this model required 2 yards of 54"-wide fabric, plus 1 yard of contrasting fabric for welting.
Cable cord
Thread to match

TECHNIQUES

Refer to Part Three for information on measuring, calculating yardage, pin fitting, and basic sewing techniques

MEASURE, MARK, AND CUT

Note: Calculate width of bias strips for welting to be sufficient for making French fold bias (refer to page 108).

(A) **INSIDE BACK/SEAT**
(B) **FRONT SKIRT**
(C) **OUTSIDE BACK/SIDE SKIRT** ✂ cut 2, reversing 1
(D) **BIAS STRIPS** ✂ cut 4" wide, to go around inside back/seat edge and lower edge of cover, including up and down each slit
(E) **BACK UNDERLAP**

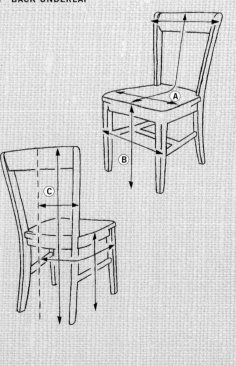

simple welted cover-up

2 Unpin the inside back/seat from the other pieces and set aside. Sew the skirt side front seams and the center back seam as marked in step 1. Press the seams open.

3 From the bias strips (D) make enough welting to trim the perimeter of the inside back/seat and the lower edge of the slipcover, including the slits, as well as the lower edge of the back underlap (refer to Basics, page 117). Referring to the Designer Detail at right, also make two 18"-long corded ties.

TIPS FROM THE PROS

✄If you make French fold bias (refer to Basics, page 108), the welting will have a neat finished edge and serve as a facing.
✄Pin and sew French fold welting to your project with the folded edge of the flange uppermost.

4 Beginning and ending on a side edge, pin welting around the right side of the inside back/seat, clipping the flange at the corners and finishing the ends neatly. Sew the welting in place. ▽

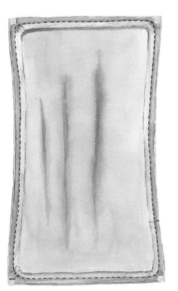

5 With the right sides together and cut edges aligned, pin a corded tie to each edge of the center back slit at the seat-height marks; baste.

6 Beginning and ending on a lower back edge, pin a continuous length of welting to the right side of the outside back/side skirts; ease the welting around the lower corners and pass it up and down each slit edge. To release tension where the welting turns at the top of each slit, remove a few stitches from the bias covering and cut completely through the cording inside it. ▽

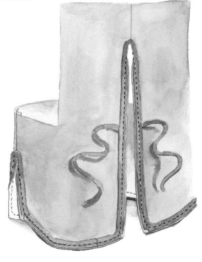

7 Beginning at the top of one slit, sew the welting in place; when you reach the top of the next slit, stop stitching. Resume stitching on the other side of the slit, and continue in this manner until all the welting is sewn on.

Attention to detail assures that even the most simply shaped covers are interesting from every angle. Here a back slit with a cording tie adds character.

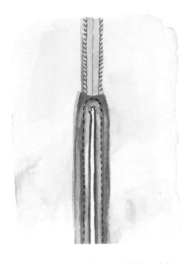

8 Place the outside back/side skirts wrong side out on your ironing board. Fold and press the welting flange onto the fabric, rolling the cord so it rims the edge. Lay each slit flat on the board and bring the corded edges together. Clip the welting flange at the top of the slit and press flat; if necessary, tug gently on the welting to ease the cord down inside the bias covering and further release the tension. △

9 Staystitch the seamline of each inside corner on the outside back/side skirts. Clip. Pin and stitch the inside back/seat to the outside back/side skirts. Press the seam; trim and clip the bulk from the seam as necessary.

10 Sew welting to the bottom edge of the underlap (E). Roll the corded edge down and press the flange up to the wrong side. Finish the side edges.

11 Put the cover on the chair wrong side out. Aligning the top edges, center the underlap, wrong side out, over the center back seam; pin. Check that the hems align. Sew together on the top seamline. ▷

12 Turn the slipcover right side out and press. Finish the end of each tie by tying in a decorative knot; trim the excess close to the knot.

covered **cording**

Covered cording can be used as a decorative trim or to make ties. The technique is a bit tricky, but once you get the hang of it, it's easy. After the cording is turned, you can leave the cord itself inside or pull it out to leave a flat tube. For each length of covered cording you wish to make, cut a piece of cord twice the desired finished length. You must use bias strips for the covering.

TIPS FROM THE PROS
✄Don't try to make more than a 3' length at one time; if you need more, make several individual lengths.
✄Making covered cording from napped fabrics such as velveteen is difficult because they stick to the cord, so are hard to turn. Try using rattail instead of cotton cable cord, and don't cover it too tightly.

1 Place the zipper or piping foot on your machine, positioning it to the left of the needle.

2 Wrap the bias strip wrong side out around the cord, placing one end of the bias at the midpoint of the cord.

3 Sew across the end of the strip, sewing through the cord and for a couple of stitches beyond it. Pivot and, stitching close to the cord, continue sewing until the rest of the cord is enclosed. ▽

4 Turn the bias right side out over the cord: Begin at the middle, where the bias is stitched across the cord. Trim the seam allowance at this point and

then, using your fingers, ease the bias gently over itself toward the exposed cord. Once the bias turns over the crosswise seam, hold the cord extending from the open end of the bias firmly in one hand and, with your other hand, continue to ease the bias down over itself; the bias will slide easily over the remainder of the cord. ▽

5 Trim the excess cord close to the stitched end.
✄If you wish to close the opposite end of the cording, cut the cord about $1/4$" inside the end, hand gather the bias covering and tuck it inside, pulling the gathers tight.
✄If you wish to remove the cord, clip off the closed end and pull the cord itself out from inside.

ruffled bistro chair cover

MATERIALS

Fabric: Shown in tiny gingham check with plaid ruffle, this model required ³/₄ yard of 54"-wide gingham and ²/₃ yard of 54"-wide plaid.

Rickrack

Thread to match

TECHNIQUES

Refer to Part Three for information on measuring, calculating yardage, pin fitting, and basic sewing techniques.

MEASURE, MARK, AND CUT

Note: For pieces B and C, cut identical pieces from outer fabric, batting, and lining. The fullness of the ruffle shown is twice the length of the corresponding slipcover edge.

Ⓐ **RUFFLES** ✂cut 4" deep, enough to go around bottom edge of back cover and outer edge of seat cover in desired fullness

Ⓑ **BACK** ✂dashed foldline corresponds to top edge of chair back

Ⓒ **SEAT**

Ⓓ **TIES** ✂cut 8, 2" x 18" each

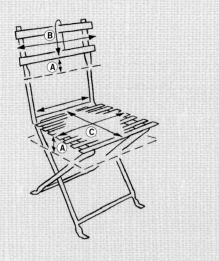

RUFFLES

1 Finish the ends of each ruffle piece (A). Sew the pieces together to make one long strip. ▽

2 Finish the bottom edge of the ruffle strip. Press the hem allowance to the wrong side. Referring to the Designer Detail on page 44, add rickrack to the hem.

3 From the ruffle strip, cut an appropriate length for each edge of the slipcover, including hem allowance on each end of each length.
✂Cut one length for each bottom edge of the back cover.
✂Cut one length for the seat back edge between the posts.
✂Cut one length for the seat side/front/side edge between the posts.

4 Hem each end of each ruffle length.

5 Gather the top edge of each ruffle length (refer to Basics, page 114).

BACK COVER

1 Layer the back pieces (B) in the following order from bottom to top: lining right side down, batting, outer fabric right side up. Pin together and baste around the edge through all layers. ▽

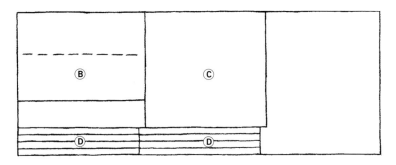

2 With the outer fabric inside, fold the back in half crosswise to form the top edge of the cover. Pin the layers together on each side edge and sew, stopping stitches 2^1/$_2$" above the bottom edges to form side slits. Press the seam allowance open, pressing it to the wrong side along the edges of the side slits. ▷

3 Adjust the gathers on both back ruffles so that the gathered edge fits between the slit seamlines. With the right sides together and cut edges aligned, pin one ruffle to each bottom edge. At each side edge, wrap the slit seam allowance around the end of the ruffle; pin. Sew the ruffles to the back. Turn the slit seam allowances to the wrong side and press all seam allowances onto the back. With the cover right side up, stitch each bottom edge just above the seamline through all layers.

4 Make four ties (refer to Basics, page 121). Pin the cut end of each tie on the wrong side of a slide slit just above the ruffle seam, and sew in place. ▽

TIPS FROM THE PROS
✂If you are making both pieces of this slipcover, make all the ties at one time.

SEAT COVER

1 Layer the seat pieces (C) in the following order from bottom to top: batting, outer fabric right side up, lining wrong side up. Pin together.

2 Measure the thickness and depth of the chair back posts to determine the size of the corner cutouts, and mark them on the lining. Sew on the marked lines; cut away the excess fabric and clip into each corner. ▽

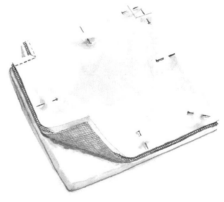

This lightly padded bistro chair cover is easy to make. If you wish to make several, set up an assembly line for fast results.

ruffled bistro chair cover

3 Turn the layers so the fabrics sandwich the batting. Pin together and baste around the edge through all layers.

4 Adjust the gathers on the ruffles so that the gathered edge fits the corresponding edge of the seat (the notches do not receive ruffles). With the right sides together and cut edges aligned, pin each ruffle to the seat; sew in place. ▷

5 Finish the seam allowance edges and press toward the seat.

6 Make four ties (refer to Basics, page 121). Pin the cut end of each tie on the wrong side of a corner notch just above the ruffle seam, and sew in place. ▷

rickrack picot edging

Rickrack comes in large as well as diminutive sizes. For a grown-up yet lighthearted effect, choose one that is bold and let it peek from behind an edge instead of stitching it on top. To begin, press the hem allowance to the wrong side of your project, but don't pin or stitch the hem until the trim has been applied.

1 Place the project right side up and open out the pressed hem. Center the rickrack over the bottom crease so the peaks extend evenly on each side. Pin or baste in place. Topstitch on the creaseline. ▽

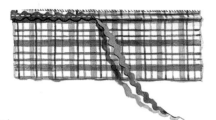

2 With the right side of the project up, refold the hem so that half of the rickrack extends beyond the crease; press. Edgestitch to hold the rickrack in place. ▽

3 If your hem allowance is deep, stitch the top edge in place as appropriate for your project.

The triangular edge of the rickrack gives these ruffles a bright and witty finish.

Simple pieces of furniture, such as this lightly upholstered armchair, look well in spare, uncomplicated slipcovers.

TIPS FROM THE PROS

✄Mark the skirts when laying out your slipcover, but don't cut them until the body of the slipcover is assembled—you'll be able to double-check their width and length and cut them accurately when you need them.

1 Lay the inside back/seat/front (A) over the inside back and seat of the chair; anchor it to the top of the chair back. Push the fabric against the top of the chair's arms and crease at the back of each to mark the seamline. In front of each crease, cut the fabric from the outside edge to the inside of the arm, then cut upward to the crease. Smooth the remainder of the fabric onto the back, seat, and front, folding the excess back as shown. Lay an arm band (B) on each arm and pin the back edge to the crease. ▽

MATERIALS

Fabric: Shown in neutral linen, this model required 3 yards of 54"-wide fabric.

Thread to match

TECHNIQUES

Refer to Part Three for information on measuring, calculating yardage, pin fitting, and basic sewing techniques.

MEASURE, MARK, AND CUT

Note: Layout shown is for nondirectional fabric; arrows indicate vertical dimension of pieces.

Ⓐ **INSIDE BACK/SEAT/FRONT**

Ⓑ **ARM BAND** ✄cut 2

Ⓒ **INSIDE ARM** ✄cut 2

Ⓓ **SIDE** ✄cut 2

Ⓔ **TOP BAND**

Ⓕ **OUTSIDE BACK**

Ⓖ **FRONT SKIRT** ✄add 2½" side and bottom hem allowance

Ⓗ **SIDE SKIRT** ✄cut 2, add 2½" side and bottom hem allowance

Ⓘ **BACK SKIRT** ✄add 2½" side and bottom hem allowance

sleek tailored cover

2 Pin an inside arm (C) to the inner edge of each arm band. Then pin each inside arm to the inside back/seat/front. Trim any excess back/seat/front fabric. Pin the remainder of the arm band to the seat front. ▽

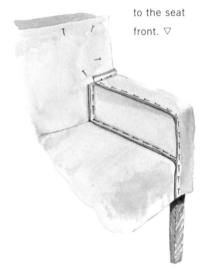

3 Rounding corners where necessary, pin the remaining pieces together as follows:
✂Anchor a side (D) to the outside of the chair and pin to the corresponding arm band; repeat with the other side.
✂Pin the top band (E) to the top edge of the back/seat/front and to the sides.
✂Anchor the outside back (F) to the outside of the chair and pin to the top band and the sides. ▷

4 Mark the seamlines and trim the excess seam allowance. Remove the slipcover from the chair. Sew it together, sewing the seams in the order in which they were pinned.

5 Place the slipcover right side out on the chair. Check the width of each skirt (pieces G, H, I) by measuring the corresponding edge of the cover, and adjust if necessary.

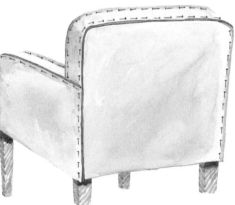

6 Referring to the Designer Detail, opposite, hem the sides and bottom of each skirt; fold the hem allowance to the right side of the skirt and sew a miter at each corner.

The linen chosen for this slipcover has neither a right nor wrong side, so we were able to turn the hem allowance to the outside for maximum effect.

7 With the rights sides together, pin each skirt to the bottom edge of the slipcover. Double-check the length, then sew in place. ▽

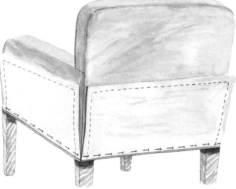

perfect mitered hems

Mitered corners give hems a neat, tailored appearance. The miters are not difficult to sew, but keeping the top and bottom folds of the hem perfectly straight and parallel can be challenging. Pressing them over a template assures crisp perfection. The width of the template should equal the finished hem depth (2" for this project); make the template as long as convenient. Tagboard is the ideal template material, whereas manila folders offer an easy source.

TIPS FROM THE PROS

✄For best results, use a straightedge and craft knife or rotary cutter when cutting your template.

✄To turn the hem to the wrong or inside of your project, exchange the terms *right side* and *wrong side* in these directions.

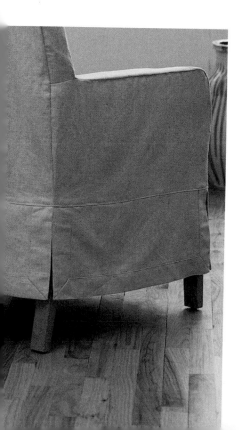

1 Cut a 2"-wide template. Draw a line parallel to and ¹/₂" from one long edge. ▽

2 Place the piece to be hemmed right side up on your ironing board. Place the template on it with the edge with the drawn line closest to the cut edge of the fabric. Fold the cut edge of the fabric over the template, aligning it with the drawn line, and press the fold to form a crease. Reposition the template and repeat until ¹/₂" has been pressed up on all hem edges. ▽

3 With the template inside the crease, fold the fabric and the template to the right side. Press the new fold to form a second crease parallel to the first. Reposition the template and repeat until this additional 2" has been pressed up on all hem edges. Unfold, revealing creaselines.

A neatly mitered hem adds subtle polish where applied trim might be too important.

4 Keep the fabric right side up. Using a small 45-degree triangle, mark a diagonal line across each corner at the intersection of the inner creaselines. ▽

5 At each corner, fold the fabric diagonally, right side out, aligning the adjacent cut edges (fold along the dash line in the drawing above). Pin together on the line drawn in the last step, and sew between the inner and outer creases only. Trim the excess fabric at the point. ▽

6 Press the mitering seams open, re-pressing the first creaseline as you do so. Turn the hem right side out, push out the points, and press each corner flat. Pin, baste if necessary, and edgestitch along the inner crease.

casual couch cover

Darts, tucks, and ties threaded through buttonholes control the fit of this cover.

MATERIALS

Fabric: Shown in cotton damask, this model required 9 yards of 55"-wide fabric.

Thread to match

TECHNIQUES

Refer to Part Three for information on measuring, calculating yardage, and basic sewing techniques.

MEASURE, MARK, AND CUT

Note: Fabric panels are sewn together to make one large rectangle. Measure your couch from floor to floor in each direction, then calculate the size to make each panel. Include allowance for tuck-in, if appropriate, and extra length and width to drape on floor as desired.

(A) **PANELS** ✂cut 3, or as needed

(B) **TIES** ✂cut 4, 4" x 55" each

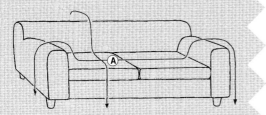

1 Sew the panels (A) together.

2 Lay the joined panels over the couch, wrong side up. Distribute the fabric evenly, tucking it into the crevice between the seat, back, and arms, and extending it evenly all around onto the floor. There will be extra fullness at the front of the arms and the side back. ▽

3 At the front of each arm, pull the fabric away from the couch and beginning about 4" below the top of the arm, pinch and pin it into a vertical dart. Pin to about 6" above the floor; the dart should be 4" to 5" wide at the bottom pin. ▷

4 In the same way, pin a dart on each side at the back of the arm. Remove the fabric from the couch and sew the darts where pinned.

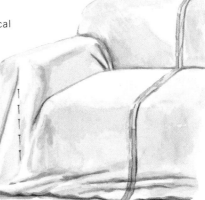

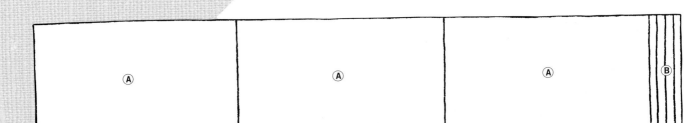

5 Place the slipcover on the couch right side up, and arrange as before. On each side of each dart, pull the fabric away from the couch, pinching a vertical tuck into the excess. Mark a buttonhole to carry each tie by placing a pin through both layers of each tuck about 1" from the fold; refer to the photos for placement. Align the folded edge of each tuck with the dart to check that the drape is pleasing. Pin the tucks over the darts temporarily. ▷

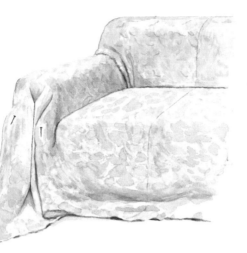

Very little fitting or sewing experience is needed to make this informal slipcover.

6 Mark the hem, rounding the corners or leaving them square as desired. Remove the slipcover from the couch. Trim the hem allowance to the desired depth. Hem the slipcover (if you wish to miter the corners, refer to the Designer Detail on page 47). Make a 1½" vertical buttonhole through each tuck where pin-marked.

7 Make four 1"-wide ties (refer to Basics, page 121), finishing all edges. Place the slipcover on the couch. Slip a tie through the pair of buttonholes over each dart and tie in a casual bow.

padded tie-on covers

MATERIALS

Fabric: Shown in cotton print, this model required 1¹/₃ yards of 45"-wide fabric, plus 1¹/₂ yards of contrasting fabric for binding and ties.
Batting
Lining
Thread to match binding fabric

TECHNIQUES

Refer to Part Three for information on measuring, calculating yardage, and basic sewing techniques.

MEASURE, MARK, AND CUT

Note: For pieces A and B, cut identical pieces from outer fabric, batting, and lining. Cut each piece to its finished dimension.

Ⓐ **SEAT**

Ⓑ **INSIDE BACK & OUTSIDE BACK** ✂cut 2

Ⓒ **TIES** ✂cut 16, 2¹/₂" x 9" each

Ⓓ **BIAS STRIPS** ✂cut 3" wide, enough to go around perimeter of each piece

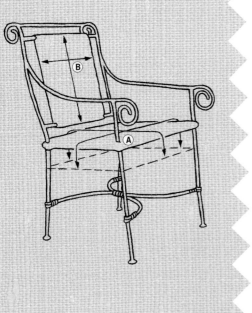

1 Layer the fabrics for the seat (A), inside back (B), and outside back (B) as follows: lining right side down, batting, and outer fabric, right side up. For each, pin through all layers in a grid pattern and baste the layers together (refer to Basics, pages 117).

2 Measure the chair seat between the posts and make a paper pattern of these dimensions. Center and pin the pattern to the lining side of the layered seat fabrics. With a pencil and straightedge, draw a line extending each side of the pattern to the edge of the fabric, marking a square at each corner. Baste the layers together just inside the central cross shape, and cut out the corners on the marked lines. ▷

TIPS FROM THE PROS

✂Be sure the corner cutouts are true squares; if they are not, the skirt hems will not align. The two front corner squares should be the same size; the two back corner squares should be the same size.

3 Referring to Basics page 121, make sixteen ties (C) 9" long. Finish one end of each.

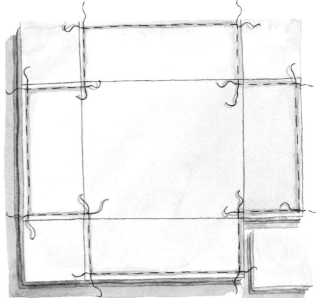

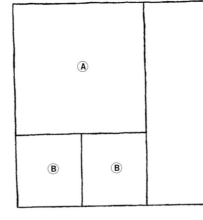

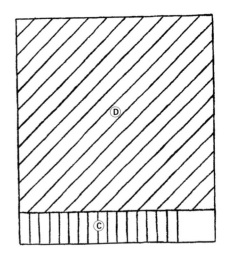

This three-piece tie-on slipcover is made just like a set of placemats. Each flat piece is lightly padded before its edges are bound.

4 Place all the pieces on the chair to determine the position of the ties. With right sides together and cut edges aligned, pin and baste two ties inside each cut-out seat corner. Also baste two ties to the top and bottom edges of the inside back and outside back. ▷

5 Referring to the Designer Detail on page 52, bind all edges of the seat and each back. Begin and end the binding at the midpoint of one edge on each piece, joining the ends neatly.

mitering binding corners

Bound edges look terrific when each corner sports a neatly stitched miter. It is not necessary to cut the miters before you apply the binding—just prepare a strip of the proper width that is long enough to go around your project, adding a couple of extra inches for ease of handling.

You must sew the binding working in one direction all the way around your project, pinning and stitching only one edge at a time. If your project has both inside and outside corners (as does the seat of our chair), sew with the binding uppermost, and work carefully around each inside corner— baste first if you wish. If your project has only inside corners, work with the project uppermost; if it has only outside corners, work with the binding uppermost (refer to Basics, page 116).

TIPS FROM THE PROS

✄When using a pieced binding strip, avoid placing the seams near the corners of your project.

✄You can make the binding any width you like. It is easiest to apply a binding whose seam allowance equals its finished width. If you wish to use an especially wide binding, and don't want to waste binding fabric in the seam allowance, mark a line on the right side of your project to which you can align the cut edge of the binding.

OUTSIDE CORNER

1 Press the binding strip in half lengthwise, right side out. Open the binding and press the cut edges to the center creaseline.

2 Open the binding on one edge. With right sides together and cut edges aligned, pin the binding to one edge of the project, pinning only to the first corner. Stitch along the creaseline, stopping the same distance from the corner as the finished width of the binding. Remove the project from the machine and cut the threads. Fold the unstitched portion of the binding away from the project at a right angle. ▽

3 Fold the binding back on itself, aligning this fold with the cut edges of the seam just stitched and the cut edge of the binding with the adjacent edge of the corner. Pin and stitch to the next corner, beginning exactly where the previous seam stopped, and stopping before the edge of the next corner as before. ▽

4 Return to the previous corner. Fold the project, wrong side out, diagonally at the corner, folding the binding away from, and the seam allowance toward, the project. On the binding, draw a diagonal line from the end of the stitching to the crosswise fold, turn 90 degrees, and draw to the outer edge of the binding— the line will be on the straight grain of the binding. Sew on the line. ◁

5 Trim the binding seam allowance from this seam, being sure to leave the corner of the project intact. ◁

6 Proceed to the next corner. If it is an outside corner, repeat steps 2–5; if it is an inside corner, see the next page. When the binding has been stitched to all edges, turn it to the wrong side of the project, encasing the cut edge. Gently push out the points at each outside corner. On the wrong side, align the folded edge of the binding with the line of stitching. Pin and slipstitch. ▽

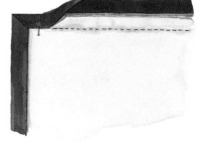

INSIDE CORNER

1 Before beginning, staystitch each inside corner, placing the stitches the width of the finished binding from the edge. At each corner, clip the seam allowance right up to the staystitching. ▷

2 Open the binding on one edge. With right sides together and cut edges aligned, pin the binding to one edge of the project.

pinning right up to the slash in the first corner. Spread the slashed corner flat and continue to pin the binding to the next corner. Stitch the pinned area. The illustrations show both sides of this seam. ▷

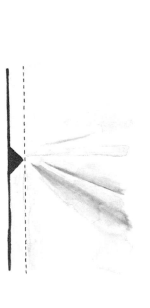

You can make your binding and ties match or contrast your main fabric. Be sure to choose a fabric that is tightly woven and not too bulky.

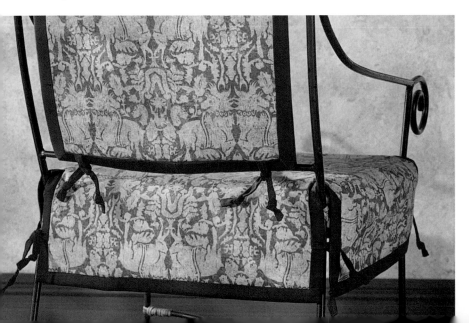

3 Return to the previous corner. Fold the project, wrong side out, diagonally at the corner, folding the binding and the seam allowance away from the project. On the binding, draw a line following the edge of the corner slash, in the middle of the binding, turn 90 degrees, and draw to the outer edge at the crosswise fold—the line will be on the straight grain of the binding.

Sew on the line. ▽

4 Trim the binding seam allowance from this seam. ▽

5 Proceed to the next corner. If it is an inside corner, repeat steps 2–4; if it is an outside corner, follow the directions on the preceding page. When the binding has been stitched to all edges, turn it to the wrong side of the project, encasing the cut edge. On the wrong side, align the folded edge of the binding with the line of stitching. Pin and slipstitch. ▷

daybed cover-up

MATERIALS

Fabric: Shown in print cotton, this model required 5³/₄ yards of 54"-wide fabric.
Thread to match

TECHNIQUES

Refer to Part Three for information on measuring, calculating yardage, and basic sewing techniques.

MEASURE, MARK, AND CUT

Note: For mattress slipcover, add seam allowance to ends, hem allowance to sides. For bolster slipcover, measure circumference and subtract amount desired for separation along tied edges, then add hem allowance to all edges.

Ⓐ **MATTRESS SLIPCOVER**
Ⓑ **MATTRESS TIES** ✂cut 12, 3" x 22"
Ⓒ **BOLSTER SLIPCOVER** ✂cut 2
Ⓓ **BOLSTER TIES** ✂cut 12, 3" x 17"

MATTRESS SLIPCOVER

1 With right sides together, sew the ends of the mattress slipcover (A) together. Press the seam open. ▽

2 Press under the hem allowance on each open edge and topstitch or blind hem, as you wish. ▽

3 Make twelve ties (B), turning in all edges of each (refer to Basics, page 121). Arrange the slipcover with the seam at one end. On the wrong side of the cover, mark the midpoint on each open edge, then mark the points halfway between it and each end. Pin a tie at each mark, aligning one end with the top of the hem. Topstitch the pinned end of each tie securely to the cover. ▷

To get the full effect of this design, choose a slipcover fabric that contrasts the mattress and bolster. To cover them first, refer to the Tips below and opposite.

TIPS FROM THE PROS

✂If the ends of your mattress are not covered by the daybed ends, before marking the tie placement, shift the slipcover seam so it will fall on one lower corner of the mattress.

✂If you wish to make an undercover for your mattress, follow the directions for making a boxed cushion cover included in the sofa slipcover, pages 58–61, omitting the welting.

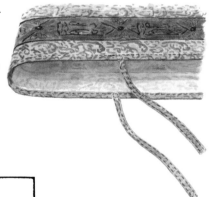

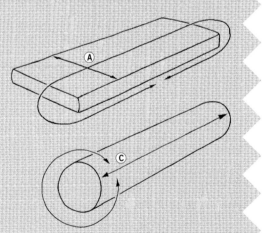

One seam and some hems and topstitched ties are all that's required to make this easy slipcover. Your fabric choice will set the mood.

BOLSTER SLIPCOVER

1 Press under the hem allowance on the ends (short edges) of each bolster slipcover (C) and topstitch or blind hem, as you wish. Then hem the sides (long edges) in the same manner.

2 Make twelve ties (D), turning in all edges of each (refer to Basics, page 121). On the wrong side of each cover, mark the midpoint of each long edge, then mark a point about 6" from each end. Pin a tie at each mark, aligning one end with the top of the hem. Topstitch the pinned end of each tie securely to the cover. ▷

TIPS FROM THE PROS

➤If you wish to make an undercover for your bolster, cut two circles the diameter of the bolster plus seam allowances and one rectangle the length by the circumference of the bolster, plus seam allowances. Press under the seam allowance on the long edges of the rectangle and staystitch the seamline on each end. With the right sides together, pin and sew each end of the rectangle to the edge of a circle, clipping the rectangle seam allowance as needed to follow the curve. Turn right side out, insert the bolster form, and slipstitch the side opening closed.

ottoman wrapper

MATERIALS

Fabric: Shown in lightweight silk plaid, this model required 1¼ yards of 45"-wide fabric, plus the same amount of contrasting fabric for lining.

Twill tape for ties (under ottoman)

Decorative tassels, medallions, and cord

Thread to match

TECHNIQUES

Refer to Part Three for information on measuring, calculating yardage, and basic sewing techniques.

MEASURE, MARK, AND CUT

Note: Measure from side to side in each direction and add 4" to each dimension to make a 2"-wide return allowance under the ottoman. The cover is reversible; cut identical pieces from two contrasting fabrics.

Ⓐ COVER

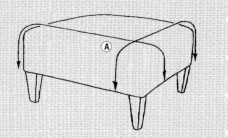

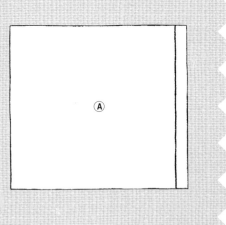

1 Measure the distance between the legs on each side of the ottoman. Center and mark this measurement on the corresponding edge of the lining (A), marking on the right side of the fabric. From the twill tape, cut sixteen pieces half the width of the ottoman, plus 6" long. (If your ottoman is rectangular, cut eight pieces for each dimension.)

2 Pin the ends of four tapes to each edge of the right side of the lining, placing two ½" inside the leg marks and spacing the others evenly between them. Baste the tapes to the edges and tack them in the center to prevent them from getting caught in the seam. ▽

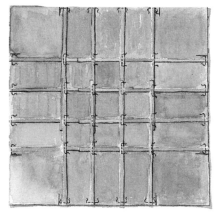

3 With right sides together and cut edges aligned, pin the contrasting fabric (A) to the lining. Sew together around four corners and three sides, leaving an opening for turning. ▷

Before wrapping the legs of the ottoman, you can fold up the corners of the cover to reveal the lining or leave them down.

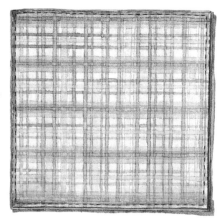

4 Trim the corners diagonally and press the seams open. Release the tacks holding the tape to the center of the lining and turn the slipcover right side out. Press the edges sharp and slipstitch the opening closed.

5 Center slipcover right side up on the ottoman; secure temporarily with pins. Turn the ottoman upside down. Tie the corresponding tapes together on the underside. ▷

Put this cover on the ottoman plaid side out, lining side out, corners up, corners down—you get multiple looks from this quick and easy design.

6 Turn the ottoman right side up. Pull each corner point down and allow vertical tucks to form on each side of each leg. Fold each corner point up and to the outside. To secure, wrap a decorative cord around the folded corner and leg; tie. Combine a decorative medallion and tassel and hand-stitch them in place. △

classic sofa cover

MATERIALS

Fabric: Shown in chenille damask, this model required 16½ yards of 56"-wide fabric.

Cable cord

Zippers for cushions

Thread to match

TECHNIQUES

Refer to Part Three for information on measuring, calculating yardage, pin fitting, and basic sewing techniques.

MEASURE, MARK, AND CUT

Note: Fabric panels are sewn together to make the deck, inside back, and outside back; cut the center panel of each the same width. Depending upon fabric and sofa, you may be able to cut the inside and outside arm as one piece. Add tuck-in allowance on adjacent edges of the seat and the inside arm and outside back as appropriate for your sofa. To the skirt width, add 16" for each pair of inverted pleats.

Ⓐ **DECK**

Ⓑ **INSIDE BACK** ✂includes top of sofa

Ⓒ **OUTSIDE BACK**

Ⓓ **INSIDE ARM** ✂cut 2

Ⓔ **OUTSIDE ARM** ✂cut 2

Ⓕ **ARM FRONT** ✂cut 2

Ⓖ **SIDE BACK** ✂cut 2

Ⓗ **BIAS STRIPS** ✂cut 3" wide, enough to go around arm fronts, side backs, perimeter of slipcover at seat level, and twice the perimeter of each cushion

Ⓘ **SKIRT** ✂cut as many panels as needed

Ⓙ **SEAT CUSHION TOP & BOTTOM** ✂cut 6

Ⓚ **BACK CUSHION FRONT & BACK** ✂cut 6

Ⓛ **CUSHION BOXING** ✂cut as many bands as needed, adding 1" extra seam allowance to cushion back or bottom boxing band depth to accommodate the slot zippers

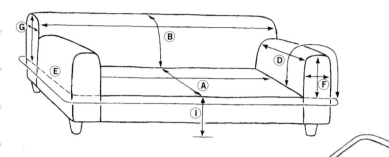

TIPS FROM THE PROS

✂Almost 4 yards of fabric were required to cut the nearly 30 yards of bias strips that were used to make the welting for this slipcover.

✂Before cutting the boxing bands for the cushions, read the cushion cover directions.

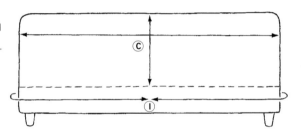

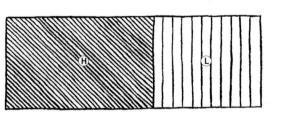

PURCHASE ONE LENGTH OF FABRIC FROM WHICH TO CUT ALL THE SLIPCOVER PIECES

This casual cover fits loosely on the sofa. You can use the same design to dress a club chair.

SOFA COVER

1 Sew together the center and side panels of the deck (A). Sew together the center and side panels of the inside back (B). Sew together the center and side panels of the outside back (C).

2 Working as follows, anchor and pin-fit the body of the slipcover on the sofa; allow for tuck-ins as appropriate:

✄Position the inside back and trim to fit around the arms. Position the deck. Pin the deck to the inside back.

✄Position the outside back and pin to the inside back. ▷

✄Pin each inside arm (D) to the corresponding outside arm (E). Position each on the sofa and pin to the adjacent edges of the deck and inside back. ▽

✄Pin each arm front (F) to the corresponding arm. ▽

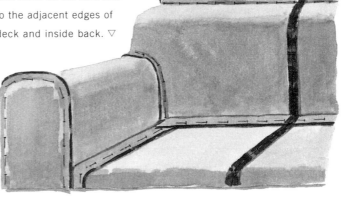

3 Complete the pin fitting of the body by pinning each side back (G) to the corresponding arm, inside back, and outside back. ▽

4 Fine-tune the fit, checking that the cover hangs below the seat level on all sides. Carefully remove the pinned pieces from the sofa. True up the seamlines, mark the seam allowances and match points, and trim the excess fabric. Disassemble the pieces.

5 Make the welting (H). Sew welting to the right side of each side back and arm front around all but the bottom edge, clipping the flange as necessary (refer to Basics, pages 117–118). ▷

6 Sew the body of the slipcover together, working in the order in which you pin-fit the pieces.

7 Place the slipcover on the sofa right side out and fold the tuck-ins onto the deck. Measure from the floor to the top of the deck and mark a line at this level all around the sofa for the skirt attachment seamline. Place the cushions on the sofa.

Inverted pleats ease the skirt around the corners. If you'd prefer your skirt to be less deep, extend the deck several inches onto the front of the sofa, extend all the other body pieces to match, and establish a lower skirt attachment line.

8 Pin-fit the skirt (I) to the sofa right side out, folding a 4"-deep inverted pleat on each side of each corner and cushion division (refer to the photo); place any seams on the inverted fold of a pleat. Mark the top seamline and the hemline. Mark a match point for each pleat on the body of the slipcover.

9 Remove the skirt and mark all the pleats, marking seamlines and seam and hem allowance where needed. Sew the skirt panels together to form a ring. Press the seams open. Hem the skirt. Clip the seam allowance above the hem. Repin all the pleats, pressing the folds and seams sharply, as shown. Baste across the top of each pleat. △

10 Sew welting to the right side of the skirt along the top seamline, beginning and ending in the center back and finishing the ends neatly (refer to Basics, pages 117–118).

11 Remove the slipcover from the sofa; mark and trim the seam allowance on the bottom edge. With the right sides together and cut edges aligned, pin the skirt to the slipcover, aligning the pleats with the match marks. Sew the skirt to the slipcover. Press the seam upward.

CUSHION COVERS

1 On the right side of each seat cushion top and bottom (J) and each back cushion front and back (K), sew welting around the perimeter, beginning and ending in the middle of the back or bottom edge, and finishing the ends neatly.

TIPS FROM THE PROS

✂ When discussing boxing bands it can be difficult to understand what is meant by the words *length* or *width*. So use the term *depth* to refer to the dimension that corresponds to the thickness of the cushion.

✂ Pin-fit one of each size cushion cover to be sure the length of its boxing band is correct.

✂ To avoid confusion, keep the pieces of the back and seat cushion covers separate.

2 Prepare the back and bottom boxing bands (L) for zippers. To do this, cut each to be 2" deeper and 1" shorter than the corresponding side of the cushion (these dimensions include ¹/₂" seam allowance). Then cut each in half lengthwise. ▽

3 Prepare the remainder of the boxing for each cushion. To do this, measure the perimeter of the cushion, subtract the length of the piece cut in step 2, and add 4" for seam allowance and zipper overlap. Cut the boxing strip to this length and 1" deeper than the cushion is thick.

4 Insert a zipper in one of the back boxing bands (refer to Basics, page 120). With the zipper closed, position the band right side up on your worktable. Fold under 1¹/₂" on one end of the corresponding side/front/side band. Overlap this end, right side up, on the zipper-pull end of the back band, aligning the cut edges. Topstitch together 1" from the fold. Using a ¹/₂" seam allowance, sew the other ends of the band together to make a ring. Repeat to make each remaining boxing band. ▽

5 Pin and sew a boxing band to a corresponding cushion top or front (refer to Basics, page 116). Open the zipper. Pin and sew the boxing to the corresponding cushion or back. ▽

6 Turn the cushion cover right side out through the zipper.

bow-trimmed slipcover

MATERIALS

Fabric: Shown in cotton chintz, this model required 3 yards of 54"-wide fabric, plus ²/₃ yard of contrasting fabric for bows and cording.

Snaps, hook and loop for back closure

Cable cord

Thread to match

TECHNIQUES

Refer to Part Three for information on measuring, calculating yardage, pin fitting, and basic sewing techniques.

MEASURE, MARK, AND CUT

Note: The skirt is attached below the top of the seat; add drop as appropriate for your chair; also add tuck-in allowance. Add 2" to width of each back for a self-facing; there is no overlap. Determine the skirt width by measuring around the chair at seat level, then add 12" for gathers and 2" each for the center back facings and top and bottom skirt hems.

- (A) **SEAT**
- (B) **INSIDE BACK**
- (C) **OUTSIDE BACK**
  - ✂ **cut 2**
- (D) **BIAS STRIPS**
  - ✂ **cut 2¹/₂" wide, enough to go around chair at seat level**
- (E) **SKIRT** ✂ **cut as many panels as needed**
- (F) **BOW** ✂ **cut 3**
- (G) **BOW WRAP** ✂ **cut 3**

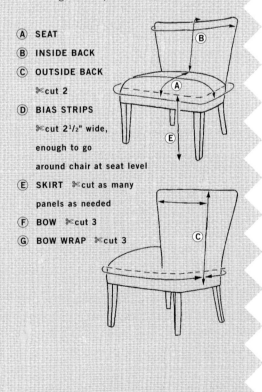

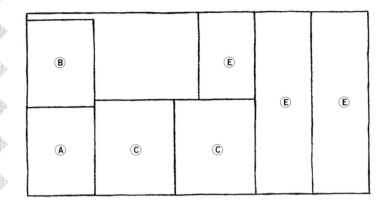

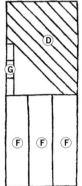

TIPS FROM THE PROS

✂ Cut the skirt with extra fullness so you can test and adjust the corner fullness on your chair.

1 Position and anchor the seat (A) and inside back (B) on the chair, allowing for tuck-in. Pin together along the back of the seat. Pin small tucks at the seat front corners and inside back upper corners. △

2 On the center back edge of each outside back (C) press 2" to the wrong side for a facing. Open the facings, align the cut edges and stitching in the aligned creases, sew the center back seam for 4" from the top. ▽

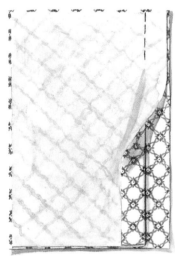

3 Refold the open facings and pin or baste to secure temporarily. Position the outside back on the chair and pin to the inside back along the top and side edges. ▽

4 Determine the level for the top of the skirt header. Measuring up from the floor, mark the skirt attachment line $1^{1}/_{4}$" below this point, all the way around the chair.

5 Carefully remove the pinned-together pieces from the chair. True up the seamlines, mark the seam allowance, and trim the excess fabric. Sew across the tucks on the seat front seamline. Sew the seat to the inside back. Sew the inside back to the outside back, breaking the seam at the tuck-in.

The skirt of this slipcover is gathered only at the corners of the seat. Tailored bows march down the center back, masking a snapped closure.

bow-trimmed slipcover

6 Sew the skirt panels (E) together to make one long strip. On each end, press under 2" to form the back self-facing. Hem the top and bottom edges. To form the skirt heading, topstitch 1¼" from the top fold.

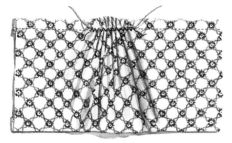

This skirt is topstitched onto the slipcover, so a deep hem was folded on the top edge to face the header above the cord and gathers.

7 Mark the seat corner placements on the skirt top edge, allowing 3" for shirring at each corner. Gather 6" of fabric at each corner (3" on each side of each mark) 1¼" below the top edge (refer to Basics, page 114). Adjust each gathered section to 3". △

8 Place the assembled seat/back pieces on the chair right side out and insert the tuck-in, butt the center back edges, and anchor. Align the skirt hem with the floor and, lapping the heading over the edge of the seat/outside back, pin together, aligning the heading topstitching with the attachment line. ▽

9 Remove the slipcover. Sew the skirt to the slipcover body. Referring to the Designer Detail on page 41, make covered cording. Hand-sew the cording over the skirt seamline, finishing the ends so they butt at the center back.

10 Referring to the Designer Detail, opposite, make three bows.

11 Pin one bow over the decorative cording at the center back. Evenly space the remaining bows above it. Tack the bows to the left side of the outside back. Sew snaps to attach the bows to the right side of the opening. Close the cover with a hook and loop under the skirt heading.

decorative **bows**

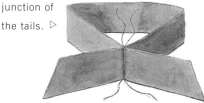

The secret to a well-composed bow is that it is not really tied; instead the center is pinched with hand stitches and then wrapped with a separate band of fabric. Make ribbon bows in the same way, omitting the turning step. Before beginning, mock-up a bow and look at it on your project to be sure the proportions are pleasing.

1 Determine the size of the finished bow so you can calculate the dimensions to which the fabric should be cut. Remember that once tied, the bow will have some dimension and be smaller than the flat strip of fabric which is used to make it.

2 For each bow, cut one strip of fabric twice as deep as the bow's finished depth and long enough to form the loops and tails, adding seam allowance to all edges. Also cut one strip for the center wrap; it should be twice the wrap's finished width plus seam allowances and long enough to wrap around the center of the bow and overlap at the ends. ▽

LENGTH

DEPTH | LENGTH

3 Fold the larger strip in half lengthwise, right side in and cut edges aligned. Cut the ends at opposite 45-degree angles. Sew from each end to the center, leaving an opening for turning. △

4 Trim the seam allowance, trimming the corners diagonally. Press the seam open and turn the piece right side out. Press the edges sharp, and slipstitch the opening closed.

TIPS FROM THE PROS
✂When pressing the seam allowance open on a narrow tube (such as the bow) that will be turned right side out later, place the tube on a small pressing board, adjust the tube so the seam is centered on it, and press, using the tip of your iron only. Avoid pressing creases into the edge of the tube, as they will be difficult to eliminate once the piece is turned.
✂If your bow is cut on the bias, press very carefully, lifting and repositioning the iron rather than sliding it along the fold—this will minimize the risk of distortion or incorrect creases along the fold.

5 Fold the long strip into a bow shape as shown (the loop portion should be slightly less than two-thirds of the strip) and pin and sew the junction of the tails. ▷

6 Refold the strip in the same way, centering the seam on the loop. With a needle and thread, tack the seam to the center of the loop by hand, then pinch the center and wrap tightly with the thread; secure with a few stitches and cut the excess thread. ▷

7 With the right side in, fold the center wrap in half lengthwise and seam the long edge. Press the seam open and turn right side out. Center the seam on the underside and press. Finish the short ends.

8 Wind the wrap around the center of the bow, overlapping the ends on the back. Tack the lapped ends together.

Wrapped tailored bows look as though they're perfectly tied.

classic skirted slipcover

MATERIALS

Fabric: Shown in cotton broadcloth, this model required 4½ yards of 54"-wide print and 2¼ yards of 54"-wide complementary solid for hem band and welting.

Cable cord

Zipper

Thread to match

TECHNIQUES

Refer to Part Three for information on measuring, calculating yardage, pin fitting, and basic sewing techniques.

MEASURE, MARK, AND CUT

Note: Add tuck-in allowance around the seat as appropriate for your chair. Determine the total skirt width by measuring around the chair at seat level and multiplying by 2, 2½, or 3 as desired. Cut the hem band to twice the finished depth plus seam allowance.

- Ⓐ **INSIDE BACK**
- Ⓑ **SEAT**
- Ⓒ **OUTSIDE BACK**
- Ⓓ **ARM** ✄cut 2
- Ⓔ **ARM FRONT** ✄cut 2
- Ⓕ **SKIRT** ✄cut as many panels as needed
- Ⓖ **BIAS STRIPS** ✄cut 2" wide, enough to edge arm fronts, back, and top of skirt
- Ⓗ **HEM BAND** ✄cut as many bands as needed

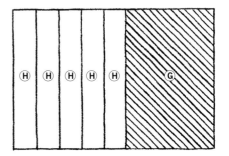

1 Working as follows, anchor and pin-fit all the pieces on the chair except the skirt and hem band; allow for tuck-ins as appropriate:

✄Position the inside back (A) and trim to fit around the arms; pin darts at the upper corners.

✄Position the seat (B) and pin to the inside back. Slash the inside corners of the T section of the seat so they will tuck in, then fold the tuck-in allowance onto the seat.

✄Position the outside back (C) and pin to the inside back. Position each arm (D) and pin to the adjacent edges of the seat, inside back, and outside back.

✄Pin an arm front (E) to each arm. ▽

2 Fine-tune the fit, checking that the intersection of the back of the arm and the outside back hangs smoothly. Carefully remove the pinned-together pieces from the chair. True up the seamlines; mark the darts, seam allowance, and match points; and trim the excess fabric from all but the bottom edges. Disassemble the pieces.

✂Reinforce the slashed inside corners of the T section of the seat with staystitching.

3 Sew the darts in the upper corners of the inside back. Sew the seat to the inside back.

4 Make the welting. Sew welting to the right side of each arm front around all but the bottom edge, clipping the flange as necessary (refer to Basics, pages 117–118). ▽

5 Sew an arm front to each arm (refer to Basics, page 116). Then sew each arm to the seat, inside back, and outside back, breaking the seams and clipping curves as necessary. Sew each arm front to the adjacent seat edge.

The skirt of this pretty slipcover hangs from the top of the seat cushion. Make it as full as you like. If you wish, you can omit the contrasting band and trim the lower edge with ribbon or braid.

6 Sew welting to the right side of the inside back/arms around the top and sides. ▽

7 Sew the outside back to the inside back, leaving one side open below the darts for the zipper.

8 Place the assembled pieces on the chair right side out and insert the tuck-ins. Pin the side opening closed. Measure from the floor to the top of the seat and mark a line at this level all around the chair for the skirt attachment seamline.

classic skirted slipcover

9 Remove the assembled pieces from the chair. Mark the seam allowance and trim any excess fabric below the skirt attachment line. Just above the line, cut the cord from inside the arm front and side/back welting. On the right side, sew welting on the skirt attachment line; stop and start the seam on each side of the tuck-in in front of each arm. △

TIPS FROM THE PROS
✄At the zipper opening edge, swing the cordless portion of the vertical welting into the seam allowance before crossing it with the horizontal welting.
✄Cut the cord from inside the horizontal welting at the side opening seamline.

10 Finish the ends of each skirt piece (F). Sew the pieces of the skirt together to make one length. Sew the pieces of the hem band (H) together to make one length. Press all the seams open.

11 Referring to the Designer Detail on page 38, attach the contrasting band to the bottom edge of the skirt. When finishing the facing in step 3, leave about 12" at each end free, pinning or basting it temporarily; it will be finished later.

12 Place the slipcover on the chair as before. Gather the top edge of the skirt (refer to Basics, page 114). Adjust the gathers and pin the skirt to the slipcover temporarily, aligning the ends of the skirt with the side opening. Check the proportion of the gathering. If the skirt is too full, eliminate the excess at this time. ▷

13 Mark match points on the slipcover and the skirt. Remove the skirt from the slipcover. With right sides together, sew the ends of the skirt together, leaving about 8" open at the top for the zipper. Sew the remainder of the hem band facing to the inside of the skirt.

14 Remove the slipcover from the chair. With the right sides together, pin and sew the skirt to it, stopping and starting the seam at the tuck-in as before. Press under the seam allowance on the edges of the zipper opening.

15 Insert a zipper in the opening so that when closed the zipper pull is at the bottom (refer to Basics, page 120).

The diagram shows labeled pattern pieces (A), (B), (D) (D) (D) (D) (D) (D) (D), and (C).

To accommodate the exposed arm of this bench, the slipcover skirt is sewn to the seat front only, then snapped to the sides and back.

1 On the bench, pin-fit the inside back/seat (A) and outside back (B) together along the top, marking the openings for the posts.

MATERIALS

Fabric: Shown in cotton broadcloth, this model required 3¼ yards of 54"-wide fabric.

Snaps

Thread to match

TECHNIQUES

Refer to Part Three for information on measuring, calculating yardage, pin fitting, and basic sewing techniques.

MEASURE, MARK, AND CUT

Note: Include the thickness of the back in the width and length measurements. This slipcover is open from the top of the arm to the front arm post; allow at least 2" allowance on the side and bottom edges of the inside back/seat and the outside back for self-facings and underlaps. The skirt has a center back opening. It is sewn to the front of the slipcover only and wraps around the rest of the bench; snaps secure the wrapped portion to the cover.

(A) **INSIDE BACK/SEAT**

(B) **OUTSIDE BACK**

(C) **ARM FACING** ✂cut 4

(D) **SKIRT** ✂cut equal amounts for skirt and lining

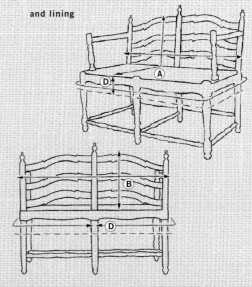

skirted open-arm cover

2 Pin the pieces together along the sides from the top to the seat, making a Y-slash to fit the inside back around each arm (refer to Basics, page 111). At the point where the back and seat meet, slash piece A up to the seamline and smooth it over the seat. Make a Y-slash to fit the seat around the arm posts. At each front seat corner, pin a dart. △

3 Mark a line following the top edge of the seat all the way around the cover. Remove the pinned pieces from the bench. True up and mark the seamlines and trim the excess fabric from the darts only. Disassemble the pieces. Staystitch the seamlines of the Y-slashed cutouts.

4 Cut a rectangular facing (C) for each arm and post cutout, making each 2" larger than the corresponding Y-slashed area. Finish the edges of each facing. Place each facing over a slashed cutout, right sides together, and stitch together following the staystitching. Slash the facings and trim the seam allowances. ▷

5 Turn the facings to the wrong side, press, and topstitch. Sew the darts at the front corners of the seat. Press the seam allowance open.

6 Pin the inside back to the outside back along the top seamline; continue pinning down each side to the top of the arm cutout. Sew together on the seamline, breaking the seam at each post opening. ▷

This slipcover would look just as charming on an armchair as it does on this bench. Or, to adapt it for a side chair, omit the arm and post cutouts and side openings.

skirted open-arm cover

7 On the outside back, even with the bottom of the arm cutout, slash the fabric from the cut edge to the seamline. Press the top seam open. Press the side seam open from the top to the slash. From the right side of the cover, topstitch around each top post opening. Also topstitch the edge of the outside back along the fold above the slash. △

TIPS FROM THE PROS

✄ If the front legs of your bench extend slightly above the seat, pad the seat with a piece of foam.

✄ It is a good idea to reinforce slashes that are not finished with a facing. To do this, fuse a piece of interfacing to the wrong side of the slash, and duplicate the slash on the interfacing. Finish the cut edges of the slash with a wide, close zigzag stitch, adding a bar tack to the apex.

8 On each side of the inside back, press under the side seam allowance between the arm cutout and seat slash, forming a facing. Topstitch along the fold.

9 Determine the number and shape of the scallops for the skirt so that a notch between scallops is placed at each corner of the seat; also plan an opening at or near the center back, adding one scallop for an underlap. Sew the skirt pieces (D) together to form one long strip. Repeat for the skirt facing pieces.

TIPS FROM THE PROS

✄ When planning the scallop size and placement, draw a scale diagram of the skirt and mark the seat corners and center back on it. Draw in the scallops, adding one for an underlap. Then mark the position of the skirt seams—center one panel across the front of the skirt and place any seams at the center of a scallop.

✄ If your scallops do not divide perfectly into each edge of the seat, make a small adjustment to the scallop size at the center of these edges—either make the center scallop(s) a bit bigger or smaller than the others, or make the center notch(es) more or less steep than the others.

10 Referring to the Designer Detail, opposite, make the scalloped skirt.

11 Place the assembled slipcover on the bench wrong side out. Pin the side openings closed and check that the line following the seat edge is correctly aligned on the front and back; remark it if necessary. Unpin and remove the slipcover. Transfer the line to the right side of the fabric with basting stitches. Determine the midpoint of the seat front edge, and mark with basting.

12 Place the slipcover on the bench right side out. At the side openings, lap the inside back over the outside back below the arms and pin. Lap the front of the skirt over the front edge of the slipcover, matching midpoints and aligning the top edge of the skirt with the basted line. Pin together across the front and on each side to the arm post cutout. Remove the slipcover and stitch the layers together close to the top edge of the skirt.

13 Place the slipcover on the bench. Pin the side openings closed as before. Wrap and pin the remainder of the skirt around the bench. Mark the placement for snaps on the side openings, along the top edge of the skirt, and at the skirt overlap, placing them about 4" apart.

14 Remove the slipcover, sew on the snaps, and remove the basting threads.

scallop-edged **borders**

You can add a scalloped border of nearly any depth to a project. Just be sure to allow a space at least the depth of your seam allowance above the notch peaks so you'll be able to turn in the top edge. To make the scallops turn smoothly, sew on a separate lining or facing; don't try to turn up a hem.

1 Make a template with a repeat of three scallops to use as a pattern: Cut a strip of tagboard or other heavy paper as wide as the scallop repeat and as high as the border depth; do not include seam allowance. Draw the scallop pattern on the tagboard; mark the midpoint of the center scallop on the top and bottom edge; cut out the template. ▷

2 On the wrong side of the pieced border fabric, draw the seamline parallel to the top edge. Mark the midpoint of the border strip on the top and bottom edges. Center the scallop template on the border, matching midpoints and aligning the top edge of the template with the marked seamline. Draw around the bottom of the template to mark the scallops. Reposition the template to one side and repeat. Continue to reposition and draw around the template until the appropriate number of scallops have been marked on each side of the midpoint.

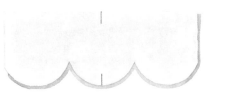

3 With right sides together and cut edges aligned, pin the border fabric to the lining, pinning along the marked seamlines. Sew along the marked lines, pivoting at each notch and corner and leaving an opening for turning at one end. Trim the seam allowance and clip each notch to the stitching line. ▽

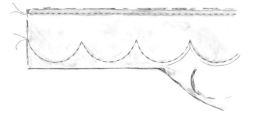

4 Turn the border right side out and press the edges sharp. Slipstitch the opening closed.

TIPS FROM THE PROS

✂ To make the peaks between the scallops turn nicely but securely, do not stitch a sharp V at each point—take one stitch across the point instead.

✂ Trim the seam allowance along the scallops close to the stitching, but avoid notching the curve. Layer the allowance.

✂ This method prepares the border for topstitching onto your project. Depending upon how you plan to use your border, you might prefer to leave its top edge open. This will allow you to insert the seam allowance of the adjacent piece between the layers of the border.

✂ If you wish to sew on the border level with the notch peaks, you can, but the seam must then be pressed away from the border. Such a treatment is unsuitable for this application, where the top edge must be faced.

Faced scallops hang smoothly around the seat of the bench.

wing chair cover

MATERIALS

Fabric: Shown in printed textured cotton, this model required 6¼ yards of 54"-wide fabric, plus 1½ yards of 54"-wide fabric for lining.

Decorative cording (with a flange)

Fusible interfacing

Buttons

Zipper for cushion

Thread to match

TECHNIQUES

Refer to Part Three for information on measuring, calculating yardage, pin fitting, and basic sewing techniques.

MEASURE, MARK, AND CUT

Note: The back button-tabs are cut in one with the outside back. Add a 4" underlap to the back edge of the outside wings and sides for a button stand and self-facing. Add a 2" overhang to the front and side-front edges of the deck. Add tuck-in allowance on adjacent edges of the inside back and inside wing, and of the deck, arm, arm front, and inside back as appropriate for your chair.

Ⓐ **DECK**

Ⓑ **INSIDE BACK**

Ⓒ **OUTSIDE BACK** ✂**cut an identical piece from lining fabric**

Ⓓ **OUTSIDE WING** ✂**cut 2**

Ⓔ **SIDE** ✂**cut 2**

Ⓕ **INSIDE WING** ✂**cut 2**

Ⓖ **INSIDE ARM** ✂**cut 2**

Ⓗ **ARM FRONT** ✂**cut 2**

Ⓘ **FRONT BAND** ✂**cut an identical piece from lining fabric**

Ⓙ **CUSHION TOP & BOTTOM**

Ⓚ **BOXING BAND** ✂**cut as many bands as needed**

TIPS FROM THE PROS

✂To assure that you understand how this cover will work on your chair, pin-fit and sew a muslin mock-up before cutting your fabric.

✂Before cutting the boxing bands for the cushions, read the cushion cover directions.

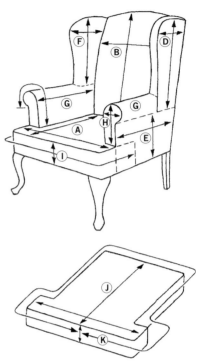

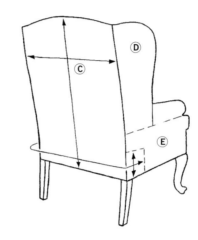

CHAIR COVER

1 Working as follows, anchor and pin-fit all the pieces on the chair except the front band; allow for tuck-ins as appropriate:

✂Position the deck (A), leaving a 2" overhang around the front edges. Slash the inside corners of the T section so they will tuck in, then fold the tuck-in allowance onto the deck. Pin a dart miter to box each front corner.

✂Position the inside back (B) and pin it to the deck.

✂Position the outside back (C) and pin it to the inside back along the top. Position the outside wings (D) and sides (E), leaving 4" extending on the back edge of each. Pin each outside wing to the adjacent side.

✂Position each inside wing (F) and pin to the adjacent outside wing, shaping the upper corners of the inside wing with tucks.

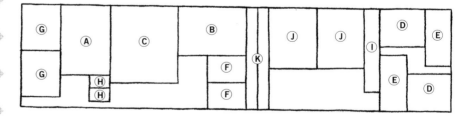

✂Pin each inside wing to the inside back, shaping the seam over the top of the back and wing as necessary and tapering the seam to allow a slight tuck-in as you pin from the top to the deck.

✂Pin each outside wing/side to the outside back. Trim the excess fabric above the buttonhole tab on each side of the outside back.

✂Pin an inside arm (G) to the top edge of the corresponding side. Smooth it over the top of the arm, clipping and trimming the fabric so it fits around the wing and down the inside of the arm, then pin it to the deck, inside wing, and inside back. Repeat with the other side.

✂Pin each arm front (H) to the deck and corresponding inside arm/side. ▽

Wraparound button tabs give a handsome finish to an otherwise understated design. You can use this detail on virtually any chair or sofa.

2 Fine-tune the fit. Carefully remove the pinned-together pieces from the chair. True up the seamlines, mark the dart miters, tucks, seam allowance, and match points, and trim the excess fabric. Disassemble the pieces.

TIPS FROM THE PROS

✂Be liberal with your use of match marks before disassembling the pin-fitted cover.

✂Reinforce the slashed inside corners of the T section of the deck with staystitching.

✂To keep track of how the pieces fit together as you sew, refer back to the illustration accompanying step 1.

tab and button wing chair cover

While a tapestry print is a great choice for a wing chair slipcover, this design would be terrific in many fabrications—consider a tailored solid with covered buttons, an arty abstract with contrasting cording, or a ticking or awning stripe with bias welting.

3 Stitch the dart miters at the front corners of the deck; press them open. Finish the front edges of the deck. Sew the back edge of the deck to the bottom edge of the inside back.

4 Sew decorative cording to the right side of each outside wing along the top and front edge (refer to Basics, page 117), clipping the flange if necessary. ▷

5 Sew each outside wing to the top edge of the corresponding side; do not sew across the piping flange at the front edge of each wing. Then sew the remaining portion of the top edge of each side to the corresponding edge of an inside arm. ▽

6 Sew decorative cording to the right side of each arm front around all but the bottom edge. ▽

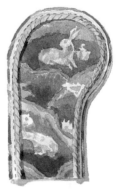

7 Sew an arm front to the front edge of each inside arm/side (refer to Basics, page 116).

8 Baste across the open end of the tucks in the upper corner of each inside wing. Sew the top/front edge of each outside wing to the corresponding inside wing; sew on the welting seamline, beginning at the adjacent seamline on the back edge of the inside wing and stopping at the bottom seamline of the inside wing. ▽

9 Aligning their back edges, sew the top of each inside arm to the bottom of the adjacent inside wing and remaining front section of the outside wing.

10 Sew each inside wing/inside arm to the adjacent side of the inside back.

11 Sew each side of the deck to the bottom of the adjacent inside arm. Then sew each T section of the deck to the bottom of the adjacent arm front.

12 Finish the back edge of each outside wing/side and press 2" to the wrong side to form a facing for the button underlaps. Place the slipcover on the chair right side out; insert the wing/back tuck-ins. Wrap the top inside back seam allowance and button underlaps onto the back of the chair and anchor temporarily with pins.

13 Pin-fit the front band (I), right side out, to the deck, aligning the top edge of the deck with the top seamline of the band; check the amount of wrap for the front buttonhole tabs. Aligning seamlines, pin the outside back to the inside back and outside wings/sides; check the amount of wrap for the back buttonhole tabs. Determine the finished length of the slipcover and measuring up from the floor, mark it on all pieces. Referring to the photographs, mark the buttonhole placement on the tabs and on each side of the outside back. ▽

14 Mark any adjustments on the front band and outside back; unpin them and remove the slipcover from the chair. Trim all the seam allowances on the front and outside back and on the bottom of the sides to the depth of the cording flange.

15 Finish the bottom edge of each side and then sew cording to it on the right side. Press the seam allowance and cording flange to the wrong side. Edgestitch through all layers, next to the cord.

16 Referring to the Designer Detail on page 79, prepare the front band and outside back. Make the buttonholes where marked (refer to Basics, page 121).

tab and button wing chair cover

17 Place the slipcover on the chair as before. Place the wrong side of the front band against the right side of the deck overhang, matching midpoints and aligning the top cording seamline on the front band with the top edge of the deck. Pin together between the front corners. △

18 Fold the inside back and outside wing/side allowances onto the chair back. Position the outside back, right side out, on the chair back, lapping it over the allowances. Align the seamlines and pin together along the top edge and for 2" down each side.

19 Remove the slipcover from the chair and sew on the outside back and the front where pinned. Sew with the slipcover right side up, stitching in the ditch of the cording seams. Trim and finish the top inside back seam allowance.

20 Sew a button opposite each buttonhole (refer to Basics, page 121).

CUSHION COVER

1 Trace the cushion shape onto the cushion top and bottom (J). Add seam allowance and cut out; staystitch and clip the inside corners of the T. On the right side of both pieces, sew decorative cording around the perimeter.

TIPS FROM THE PROS

✂When discussing boxing bands it can be difficult to understand what is meant by the words *length* or *width*. So use the term *depth* to refer to the dimension that corresponds to the thickness of the cushion.

✂Pin fit the cover on the cushion before inserting the zipper in step 4, below.

2 The zipper opening in the cushion boxing band must be long enough for the front of the T to fit through it, so it must span the cushion back and wrap onto each side. To prepare the back boxing band (K) for the zipper, cut it to be as long as the front of the cushion across the T plus 1", and 2" deeper than the cushion is thick. Cut it in half lengthwise.

3 Prepare the remainder of the boxing band. To do this, measure the perimeter of the cushion, subtract the length of the piece cut in step 2, and add 4" for seam allowance and zipper overlap. Cut the boxing strip to this length and 1" deeper than the cushion is thick.

4 Insert the zipper in the back boxing band (refer to Basics, page 120). With the zipper closed, position the band right side up on your worktable. Fold under 1¹/₂" on one end of the remaining section of the boxing band. Overlap this end, right side up, on the zipper-pull end of the back band, aligning the cut edges. Topstitch together 1" from the fold. ▽

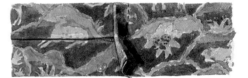

5 Sew the other ends of the band together to make a ring. Pin and sew the boxing band to the cushion top, pivoting at each corner (refer to Basics, page 116). ▽

6 Open the zipper and sew the boxing band to the cushion bottom. Turn the cushion cover right side out through the zipper.

lined button-on pieces

Practical buttons are a decorative alternative to a zipper. Consider giving the piece with the buttonholes a complete lining—you won't have to worry about securing the inside edge of a facing to the outer fabric. Cut the lining and outer fabric to be identical; if the piece is asymmetrical, reverse the lining. Be sure to allow for a faced underlap to support the buttons on the opposite edge of the opening.

1 Fuse interfacing to the wrong side of each button tab. Trim the seam allowance on the outer fabric and lining to the width of the cording flange.

2 If desired, on the right side of the piece, sew decorative cording around the perimeter; begin and end the cording in middle of the bottom edge and finish the ends neatly (refer to Basics, page 119). Be sure to ease the cording around any outside corners so it doesn't bind when right side out.

3 Place the lining right side up on a table. Place the piece with the cording over it, right side down, and cut edges aligned. Pin and sew together along the cording seam, leaving an opening for turning in the middle of one long edge.

4 Trim the seam allowance at any outside corners. If there are inside corners, clip right up to the stitching. Turn the piece right side out. Press the seam allowance along the opening to the inside, and slipstitch the opening closed.

TIPS FROM THE PROS
✂Choose a lining fabric that complements your outer fabric—you probably want something that adds body but is not overly stiff or heavy.
✂It takes less time to baste the lining to the outer fabric than it does to pick out an uneven seam.
✂Don't be timid when trimming excess bulk from corners. The seam allowance should form a miter when folded back onto the corner. ▽

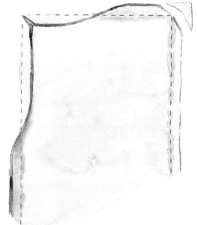

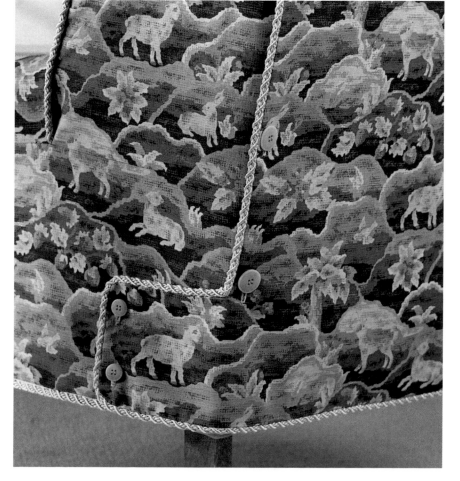

Practical buttons take the place of a zipper on this slipcover. Make the side tabs in a proportion that suits your chair.

fringed ottoman cover

MATERIALS

Fabric: Shown in cotton chintz, this model required 2¼ yards of 54"-wide fabric.
Decorative cording (with a flange)
Fringe
Thread to match

TECHNIQUES

Refer to Part Three for information on measuring, calculating yardage, and basic sewing techniques.

MEASURE, MARK, AND CUT

Note: Measure the circumference of the ottoman top where the skirt will be attached; to determine the fullness of the skirt, double or triple this measurement as you wish (refer to Basics, page 119). Add hem allowance to the bottom of the skirt.

Ⓐ **TOP**
Ⓑ **SKIRT** ✂cut as many as needed

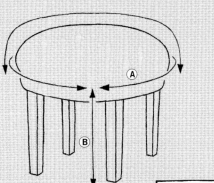

1 Center the top (A), right side up, on the ottoman. Tie a piece of narrow elastic around the ottoman where you wish to attach the skirt. Adjust the fabric fullness evenly. Using dressmaker's chalk, mark a line around the top just above the elastic. ▽

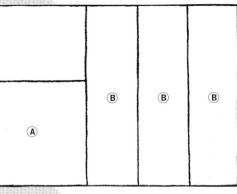

2 Untie the elastic and remove the top. Using a pencil and French curve or flexible ruler, smooth out the curved line marked in step 1. (If your ottoman is oval or because of the bias drape of the fabric, the final shape may not be a perfect circle.) Add seam allowance and cut out the top. ▷

3 Gather the top on the seamline by zigzagging over heavy thread (refer to Basics, page 114). Place it right side up on the ottoman. Pull the thread to ease the top to fit the ottoman loosely—if it is too tight, you'll have difficulty putting the finished cover on. Secure the thread ends. Adjust the fullness so it drapes attractively.

4 With the top still on the ottoman, pin the cording flange over the gathers so the cord sits just above the gathering thread. Baste, and trim the cording ends, leaving enough to finish neatly later. Remove the top and sew on the cording, finishing the ends appropriately (refer to Basics, pages 117–118).

5 Finish the ends of each skirt piece (B). Sew the pieces together to make one long strip. Hem one edge of the skirt, leaving the hem unstitched for 3" at each end; it will be completed later. Gather the top edge of the skirt.

6 Place the top on the ottoman. Adjust the gathers on the skirt and pin temporarily to the top, aligning the skirt seamline with the welting seamline. If the skirt is too full, eliminate the excess at this time. To determine the proper placement for the fringe, pin a portion of it to the skirt—because the weight of the fringe may affect its length, it is better not to do this with the skirt flat on your worktable. ▽

7 Remove the skirt, relax the gathers, and mark the fringe placement line parallel to the bottom of the skirt. Pin and sew the fringe to the skirt, leaving the fringe free for 3" at each end; it will be finished later.

8 Sew the remaining skirt seam. Complete the hem. Turn under the ends of the fringe header so they butt over the skirt seam, and slipstitch them together. Sew the loose section of the fringe to the skirt. ▽

Choose solid, striped, plaid, check, or print fabrics for this design, but avoid any patterns that would look upside down on the far side of the ottoman top.

9 Adjust the gathers evenly so the skirt fits the top. With right sides together, pin and sew the skirt to the top. Press the seam up, toward the top.

TIPS FROM THE PROS

✂If your ottoman is oval, or the upholstery slightly uneven, you may find that this cover fits best when aligned in a specific orientation. To keep it properly aligned, sew ties to the top/skirt seam above each ottoman leg, and knot them around it.

skirted
button-back cover

MATERIALS

Fabric: Shown in cotton broadcloth, this model required 1¹/₂ yards of 54"-wide print fabric, plus 1¹/₂ yards of contrasting fabric for the back and band.

Cable cord

Buttons

Thread to match

TECHNIQUES

Refer to Part Three for information on measuring, calculating yardage, pin fitting, and basic sewing techniques.

MEASURE, MARK, AND CUT

Note: Allow for thickness of chair back on the inside back piece. On the right outside back and band, add 5" for the facing and underlap on the center back edge; the left center back edge gets a separate facing. Allow for eight pairs of inverted pleats on the skirt (see the TIPS on page 84 if you are pleating a large repeat).

Ⓐ RIGHT OUTSIDE BACK

Ⓑ LEFT OUTSIDE BACK

Ⓒ INSIDE BACK

Ⓓ SEAT

Ⓔ BIAS FOR
   BUTTON LOOPS
   ✂cut 1" x 18"

Ⓕ LEFT BACK FACING

Ⓖ BIAS FOR
   WELTING ✂cut
   in appropriate width,
   enough to rim chair
   back and top and
   bottom of band

Ⓗ BAND

Ⓘ BAND FACING

Ⓙ SKIRT ✂place
   on grainline
   appropriate for
   fabric pattern

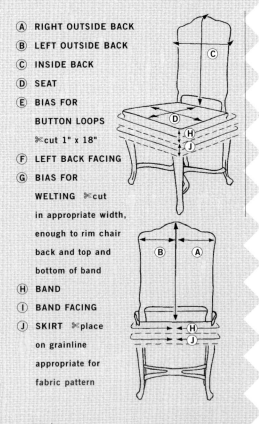

1 On the right outside back (A), press 3" to the wrong side on the center back edge. On the right side of the piece, mark the center back line parallel to and 2" from the fold. On the left outside back (B), draw the center back seamline. Overlap the pieces, aligning the center back lines, and pin.

2 Pin-fit the outside back, inside back (C), and seat (D) on the chair, centering the marked, pinned center back, shaping the top edge, and folding tucks at the upper corners of the inside back (refer to Basics, page 112). Mark the shape of the seat, and shape the intersection of the seat and inside back appropriately at the side edges. ▷

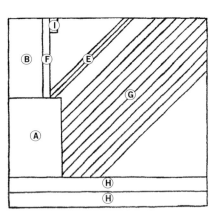

3 On the back, mark the placement of the buttons and loops as shown in the photograph, or as desired. Remove the pinned pieces from the chair, true up the seamlines, disassemble the pieces, and mark the seam allowances. Trim the excess fabric. Baste the tucks in the upper corners of the inside back.

TIPS FROM THE PROS

✂If your chair's legs have knees, measure the entire lower edge of the cover before trimming the seam allowance around the seat. Check that it is as big as the lower edge of the band should be. If it is not, add edge to the outside of the seat until it is, otherwise, your band will not hang properly.

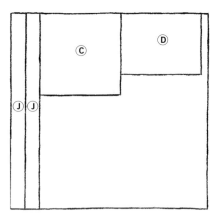

4 Make six self-filled tubular button loops (E). Follow the directions given in the Designer Detail on page 41, but wrap the bias over a very thin cord and stitch ¼" from the fold; do not trim the seam allowance from the bias and, after you turn the tubing right side out, remove the cord. Cut the tubing to the appropriate length to encircle your buttons, plus seam allowance. With right sides together and cut edges aligned, place four loops on the left outside back at the positions marked in step 3; staystitch.

5 With right sides together, pin and sew the facing (F) to the center back edge of the left outside back. Turn the facing to the wrong side and press; topstitch. To complete the right outside back edge, topstitch along the fold. Matching the centers as before, overlap the left outside back on the right outside back; baste across the top. ▽

6 Make the welting (G) and, right sides together and cut edges aligned, sew it to the right side of the outside back around the side and top edges (refer to Basics, page 117).

7 With right sides together, sew the seat to the inside back. Sew the outside back to the inside back. Turn right side out and press.

8 Sew welting to the lower edge of the cover, finishing the ends so they butt at the center back. To do this, remove about 1" of stitching at each end of the bias and open it out, cut the cord at the center back line, trim the end of the bias to ½", fold it over the end of the cord, then refold the bias and stitch the welting in place. ▷

The lines of this cover are actually quite simple, but the details give it great presence. It's fun to use an important print to enhance the effect.

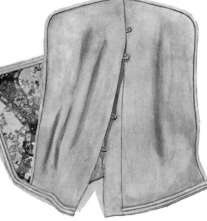

skirted button-back cover

9 Sew the pieces of the band (H) together to make one length. Determine the left center back end. Position the two remaining button loops on it, centering them between the top and bottom seamlines and spacing them as you did the other pairs of loops; baste. ▽

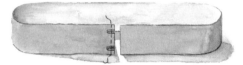

From the back, this chair is prim and proper. Using a contrasting fabric for the back and band excuses you from careful pattern matching—and looks terrific.

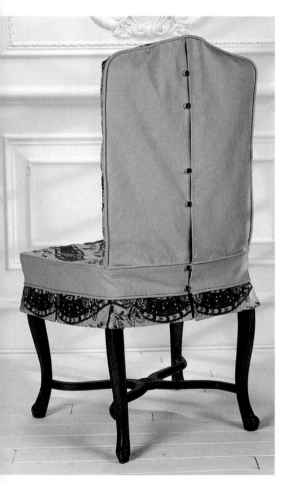

10 Finish one end of the band facing (I). With right sides together and cut edges aligned, place it over the end of the band with the loops, and sew. Turn the facing to the wrong side, press, and topstitch along the fold. Finish the other end of the band with a self-facing as on the right outside back.

11 With right sides together, sew the band to the welted bottom edge of the cover. ▷

12 Sew welting to the bottom edge of the band; finish the ends at the center back, as in step 7. On the lower edge of the band, mark the center front, the center of each side, and each corner.

13 Sew the pieces of the skirt (J) together to make one length. Hem the lower edge.

14 In the skirt, form 1½"-deep inverted pleats to align with the center front, center of each side, and each corner, as marked in step 11. Also make a knife pleat to align with the right center back edge, extending the return to the edge of the underlap. Fold each end of the skirt to the wrong side to make a facing. Baste the pleats and facings in place. ▽

TIPS FROM THE PROS

✄Form the pleats before sewing the sections of the skirt together, then hide the seams inside the pleats.

✄When pleating a skirt made from fabric with a large repeat, arrange the pattern so it falls attractively at each pleat. If the distance between the pleats is not consistent (for instance, if the sides, front, and back of the chair are different lengths) there may be no easy mathematical way to do this, so trust your eye. Begin at the center front, and work out symmetrically from there.

✄Piece the underlap of the pleats where necessary to keep the pattern attractive.

15 With the right sides together and cut edges aligned, pin the skirt to the bottom edge of band, aligning pleats with marks, and sew.

16 Sew the buttons to the right back to correspond to the button loops.

1 On one long edge of the skirt (A) press 1¹/₂" to the wrong side twice to form a double hem. Topstitch along the inner hem edge.

2 Referring to the Designer Detail on page 87, form a 1¹/₂"-deep tuck above the hem and stitch.

Whenever you double or triple the layers of sheer fabric, its color intensifies, giving details such as hems and tucks a subtle importance.

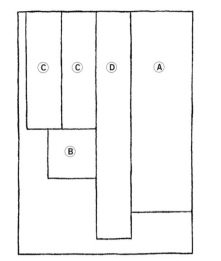

MATERIALS
Fabric: Shown in silk organza, this model required 1³/₄ yards of 45"-wide fabric.
Lining for seat
Thread to match

TECHNIQUES
Refer to Part Three for information on measuring, calculating yardage, and basic sewing techniques.

MEASURE, MARK, AND CUT
Note: Add length and width to the skirt (A) measurements to allow for pleats, tuck, and hem: To width add 15" for ten ³/₄"-deep pleats; to length add 3" each for hem and tuck—or as appropriate for the scale of your chair. Cut the ties to a length appropriate for your chair; the one-piece back tie is centered across the back edge of the seat and extends to form a tail at each corner.

Ⓐ **SKIRT**
Ⓑ **SEAT** ✂cut a matching piece from lining fabric
Ⓒ **SIDE TIE** ✂cut 2, 9" x 30" each
Ⓓ **BACK TIE** ✂cut 1, 9" x 58"

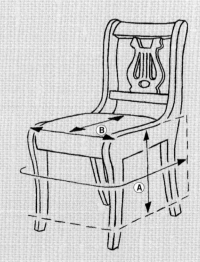

tuck-trimmed apron

3 With the right side of the fabric up, mark the midpoint of the top edge of the skirt. Evenly space three $^3/_4$"-deep pleats on each side of it; face them away from the center, positioning the outer pleats to correspond to the front seat corners. Mark the midpoint of each remaining section of the top edge and make two more pleats, facing them away from the marks. Baste across the top of each pleat. ▽

4 Make a narrow rolled hem on each end of the skirt (refer to Basics, page 115).

5 Measure the thickness and depth of the chair back posts to determine the corner cutouts for the seat (B). Place the seat and lining right sides together, mark the cutouts on the lining, and stitch. Trim the seam and clip to the corner. △

6 Turn the seat right side out and press. Baste the layers together along the cut edges.

7 With right sides together and matching midpoints, sew the top edge of the skirt to the seat front and side edges; the skirt will extend beyond the cut-out corners to align with the back edge of the seat. ▽

TIPS FROM THE PROS

✂ For the tails of a bow to align, one must be longer than the other: The longer one must wrap the center when the bow is tied. We made the side ties longer than the tails of the back tie.

✂ Bows behave best when the longest edge is cut on the lengthwise grain. If your fabric is crisp, they can be pretty when cut on the bias, but to avoid distortion, stitch carefully and do not slide the iron when pressing.

Try this design in a sturdy check or print— or use stripes, placing them horizontally on the skirt, to create a band of color with the tuck.

8 Fold each tie (C and D) in half lengthwise, wrong side out. Cut one end of each side tie and both ends of the back tie on a 45-degree angle.
✄ Stitch each side tie together along its cut edges, leaving open the square end and enough of the adjacent side to later enclose the extending skirt top edge.
✄ Stitch the back tie (D) together along its cut edges; in the center of the long edge, leave an opening equal to the width of the back edge of the seat.
✄ Trim the seams and turn the ties right side out; press. Press the seam allowances of the openings to the inside.

TIPS FROM THE PROS
✄ Before turning a lined piece right side out, press open the perimeter seam allowances—this makes it easier to press a sharp crease on the edges after the piece is turned.

9 To attach each side tie, slip the skirt extension seam allowance into the side opening and edgestitch through all layers, then fold the edge of the tie twice toward the skirt and slipstitch or zigzag its end to the cut-out edge. To attach the back tie, slip the seat back seam allowance into the back tie opening. Edgestitch through all layers. ▷

10 Press the seat front and side seam allowance toward the seat and edgestitch.

11 Place the slipcover on the chair, slipping the back tie under the chair back. Tie a bow at each back corner.

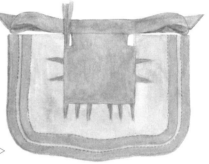

perfect **tucks**

Place simple tucks above a hem to emphasize the effect of sheer or striped fabrics. To be sure you allow enough length, follow the directions below to plan tucks before you cut the skirt. Before marking, hem the skirt (or mark the top of the hem on the right side of the fabric). Then place it flat, right side up, on a worktable. If you wish to make more than one tuck, repeat steps 1 through 4 for each, measuring from the previous tuck rather than the hem.

1 Decide how deep you wish the tuck to be. (We made the tuck on the sheer skirt 1 1/2" deep.) Decide how much space you want between the bottom of the tuck and the top of the hem. (We allowed 1/2".) Add the two measurements together (2").

2 Using a straightedge and dressmaker's chalk, mark a line parallel to and this distance from the top of the hem. Mark a line parallel to the first and twice the depth of the tuck above it. ▽

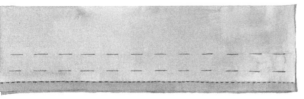

3 Fold the fabric, right side out, bringing the marked lines together, and pin. Stitch along the entire marked line. ▽

4 Place the skirt right side up on your ironing board, and press the tuck toward the hem. ▽

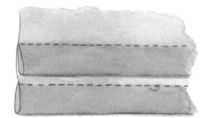

sofa cover

MATERIALS

Fabric: Shown in brocade, this model required 12 yards of 56"-wide fabric.
Decorative cording (without flange)
Tassels
Thread to match

TECHNIQUES

Refer to Part Three for information on measuring, calculating yardage, pin fitting, and basic sewing techniques.

MEASURE, MARK, AND CUT

Note: Fabric panels are sewn together to make the seat, inside back, and outside back; cut the center panel of each the same width. Divide the bottom edge of each side of the sofa for as many draped swags as you like, being sure to measure from the outermost corners of the frame. Refer to the Designer Detail on page 92 before calculating yardage.

Ⓐ **SEAT**

Ⓑ **INSIDE BACK**

Ⓒ **OUTSIDE BACK**

Ⓓ **TOP BAND** ✂cut and piece as necessary

Ⓔ **ARM BAND** ✂cut 2

Ⓕ **INSIDE ARM** ✂cut 2

Ⓖ **SIDE** ✂cut 2

Ⓗ **SWAG** ✂swag width may vary

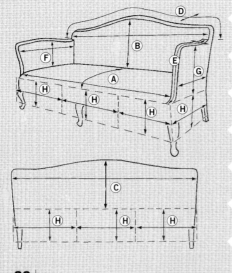

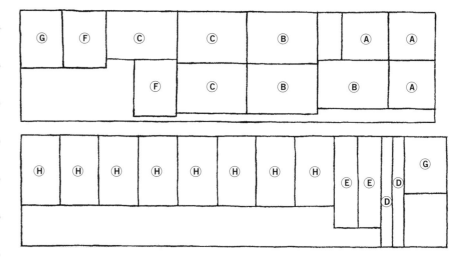

PURCHASE ONE LENGTH OF FABRIC FROM WHICH TO CUT ALL THE SLIPCOVER PIECES

TIPS FROM THE PROS

✂If your sofa has an upholstered back or arms, refer to a project that more closely resembles it while measuring, pin fitting, and sewing.

✂If your sofa arms are sinuous like those in the photo, pin-fit the arm pieces in muslin before cutting from final fabric.

1 Sew together the center and side panels of the seat (A). Sew together the center and side panels of the inside back (B). Sew together the center and side panels of the outside back (C).

2 Working as follows, anchor and pin-fit the body of the slipcover on the sofa; allow for tuck-ins as appropriate:

✂Position the inside back. Push the fabric against the top of the sofa's arms and crease at the back of each arm to mark the seamline. In front of each crease, cut the fabric from the outside edge to the inside of the arm, then cut upward to the crease. Smooth the remainder of the fabric onto the back, folding the excess back as shown.

✂Position the outside back. Position the top band (D) and pin it to the inside back and outside back, stopping at the top of each arm.

✂Position the seat and pin it to the inside back. ▽

✂Position an arm band (E) on each arm and pin the back edge to the crease on the inside back. Position the inside arms (F) and the sides (G), and pin to the adjacent arm band, contouring the arm band as necessary.

✂Pin each inside arm to the seat and inside back. Pin the remainder of each arm band to the adjacent front edges of the seat.

✂Pin each side to the adjacent end of the top band, then pin to the adjacent edge of the outside back. ▷

3 Fine-tune the fit, checking that the cover hangs below the point where you'll attach the skirt on all sides. Carefully remove the pinned-together pieces from the sofa. True up the seamlines, mark the seam allowances and match points, and trim the excess fabric. Disassemble the pieces.

Making a slipcover of this complexity is not for the faint of heart, but if you are confident of your cutting, fitting, and sewing skills, you'll find the results worth the effort.

swag-skirted sofa cover

4 On the right side of the seat, lay cording over the seams joining the panels. Allow enough extra cording at the front edge to later cover the swag seamlines and turn to the wrong side. Baste the cording in place at the back edge of the seat. ▷

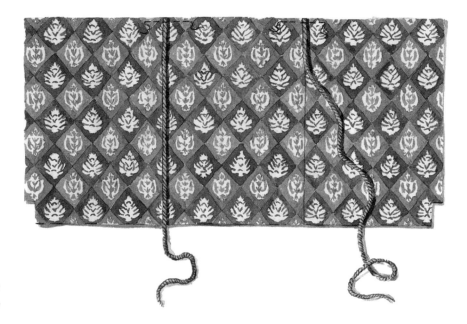

This formal design is as appealing from the back as the front, so it is a good choice for a sofa positioned away from a wall.

5 Working as follows, sew the body of the slipcover together:

❧Sew the inside back to the top band.

❧Sew the outside back to the top band.

❧Sew the seat to the inside back.

❧Sew each inside arm to the top/front edge of the corresponding arm band.

❧Sew each side to the top/front edge of the corresponding arm band.

❧Sew each inside arm to the seat, stopping at the back tuck-in.

❧Starting at the seat tuck-in and working up, pin an inside arm to the adjacent edge of the inside back, then pin the back of the arm band to the inside back; sew the seam with the inside back facing up. Repeat with the other arm.

6 Place the slipcover on the sofa right side out and insert the tuck-ins. Determine the level at which to attach the swagged skirt (H). Measure from the floor to this point and mark a line at this level all around the sofa. Divide the lower edge of the sofa for swags and mark the divisions on the line.

7 Measure and jot down the width of each swag section. Referring to the Designer Detail on page 92, make eight swags.

TIPS FROM THE PROS

❧Although you'll want the widths of your swags to appear equal or symmetrical, your furniture may be somewhat asymmetrical and each swag might actually be a different size. As you work, label each swag and arrange them in the proper sequence before sewing together.

8 Pin-fit the swags to the sofa right side out, aligning the seamlines and lapping the top edge of each over the bottom of the slipcover; adjust if necessary. Remove the swags and sew together on their adjacent edges, sewing through all layers. △

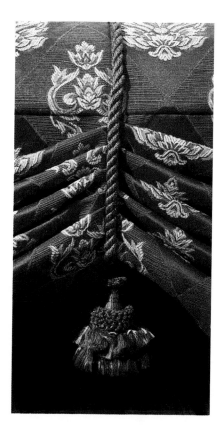

9 Remove the slipcover from the sofa. Mark and trim the seam allowance on the bottom edge. Press the seams between the swags open. With the right sides together and cut edges aligned, pin the swagged skirt to the bottom edge of the slipcover, aligning the swag seams with the match points. Sew the skirt to the slipcover. Press the seam upward.

10 Catchstitch the cording along the seamline of the seat and swags. Turn several inches of cording to the wrong side at the bottom edge and hand stitch to secure.

11 Place the slipcover on the sofa and insert the tuck-ins. Determine the position of the tassels and sew them in place.

Proportion is critical to the success of a tassel. This one is full, shapely, and appropriately stately. If you'll be custom-ordering tassels, making even a crude mock-up will help you judge the scale and avoid a costly wrong choice.

pleated swags

Swags give a dressy finish to a slipcover. You can cut them on the bias if appropriate for your fabric. If you wish to line them, do so after fitting them and before basting the final pleats. To arrange the pleats, you'll need a blocking board or other flat surface into which you can insert pins.

1 To make a swag template, experiment with a piece of muslin that is 10" wider than the finished swag and twice as long as the deepest part of the swag. Draw the top seamline $1/2$" below the top edge of the muslin. Center and mark the finished width of the swag on the line; also mark the center point. Draw vertical lines on the muslin from the marks down. Pin the top edge of the muslin to the board between the outer marks. ▽

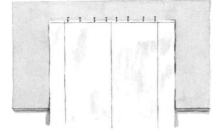

2 Beginning about 2" below the top, form the first drape, pinching a horizontal tuck about $1^{1}/_{2}$" deep on each vertical line and folding it upward. Allow the fabric to relax and curve in a pleasing manner. Moving down, form four more drapes, making each drape deeper and more relaxed than the previous one. The outer marked lines will slant inward and move toward the center of the swag; the center line should fold straight through each drape. ▽

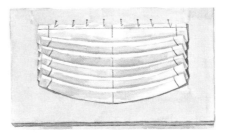

3 Mark the side seamlines, drawing a new vertical line perpendicular to the top edge at each outer mark.

4 If your drapes are pinned into the board, repin through the muslin only. Remove the muslin from the board and test it on the sofa, pinned side out; adjust if necessary. Add a seam allowance to each side and trim the excess fabric. Mark the foldlines and lap lines. Unpin the pleats. Mark a slight curve along the bottom edge and add the hem allowance.

The fabric chosen for this sample is a soft brocade that drapes easily. If you are considering chintz for this design, test it first to see if you like the way it drapes.

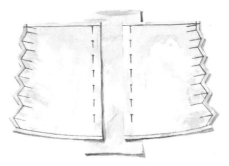

5 Use this muslin as the pattern to cut each swag. To narrow or widen a swag, cut the pattern on the center vertical line and spread or overlap the two halves the required amount. △

6 Hem the bottom edge of each swag. Pin the pleats. Baste through all layers on each seamline.

TIPS FROM THE PROS

✂The muslin mock-up you've made is pleated as the final swag should appear right side out. To easily keep track of the pleats, mark them onto the cut fabric with hand basting— this way they'll be apparent from either side.

✂Your fabric may drape somewhat differently from the muslin. Cut the swags with extra side seam allowance so you'll be able to adjust the draping if you wish.

✂If your fabric is bulky, finish the side edges of each swag before basting across the ends of the pleats. If it is lightweight, you can probably finish through all layers at once.

BACK

1 Pin-fit the inside back (A) and the outside back (A) on the chair, leaving a 4" opening at the bottom of each side. Remove the pinned pieces from the chair, true up the seamlines, and mark the top of the side openings. Disassemble the pieces, mark the seam allowances, and trim the excess fabric.

2 Hem the lower edge of the inside back.

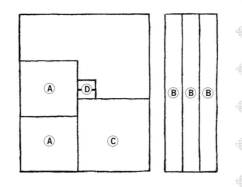

3 Referring to the Designer Detail on page 95, prepare enough of the skirt (B) to fit across the lower edge of the outside back. Plan to center one pleat (or space between pleats) and arrange the others symmetrically on each side of it, being sure to allow a narrow hem allowance at each end.

Spaced box pleats hang from the lower edges of this two piece cover. For a different look, use one fabric for the entire slipcover.

MATERIALS

Fabric. Shown in matelassé with a damask ruffle, this model required 1¼ yards of 54"-wide fabric for the covers, plus ½ yard of 54"-wide fabric for the skirt.

Decorative cording (without flange)
Thread to match

TECHNIQUES

Refer to Part Three for information on measuring, calculating yardage, pin fitting, and basic sewing techniques.

MEASURE, MARK, AND CUT

Note: Add hem allowance to the lower edge of the inside back. Be sure to include the drop on all four sides of the seat. Refer to the Designer Detail on page 95 to calculate the skirt fullness.

(A) **INSIDE BACK & OUTSIDE BACK** ✂cut 2
(B) **SKIRT** ✂cut 6" deep, enough to go across outside back and around seat when pleated
(C) **SEAT**
(D) **BACK POSTS FACING** ✂cut 2

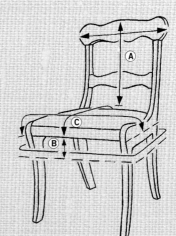

4 Pin and sew the pleated skirt to the lower edge of the outside back. ▽

5 Press the seam toward the back; topstitch if desired. Sew the inside back to the outside back along the sides and top, leaving open below each side mark. ▽

6 Finish the edges of the side openings and skirt ends and press to the wrong side; topstitch. Cut four ties from decorative cord. Sew one end of a tie inside each side opening just above the skirt. ▽

SEAT

1 Center the seat (C) on the chair wrong side up. Mark the outline of the chair seat, folding the back edge of the fabric up so you can mark the position of the back posts. Pin a dart miter at each front corner to box the seat (refer to Basics, page 112). Mark the bottom edge on the front and sides, also mark the side/back ends of the drop.

2 Remove the marked piece from the chair. True up the seamlines, checking that the corner darts are symmetrical. Mark the back post cutouts and staystitch. Mark the seam allowance and trim the excess fabric, leaving enough at the back drop to adjust later (do not trim the cutouts or the sideback corners). ▽

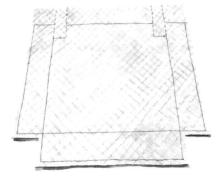

3 Pin and stitch the front corner darts. Press the seam allowance open.

4 To face the back post cutouts (D), cut two rectangles of fabric, each 2" larger than the marked area. Finish the cut edges. Place a rectangle under each cutout, right sides together, and stitch on the marked line. Make a Y-slash (refer to Basics, page 111) and turn the facing to the wrong side; topstitch. Then trim and hem the back of each side drop. ▷

5 Place the seat on the chair and double-check the length of the back drop; mark the seam allowance and trim any excess fabric.

6 Referring to the Designer Detail, opposite, prepare two pieces of the skirt, being sure to allow a narrow hem allowance at both ends of each.
✂ Make one to fit across the back drop, positioning the pleats as you did on the back slipcover.
✂ Make the other to fit around the remaining sides of the seat, positioning the pleats symmetrically and concealing any seams inside a pleat.
✂ Finish the ends of each skirt, fold the hem allowance to the wrong side, and topstitch to match the back slipcover skirt.

7 Pin and sew each skirt to its corresponding seat edge. Press the seams toward the seat; topstitch if desired. Cut four ties from decorative cording. Sew one end inside each back cutout, just above the skirt.

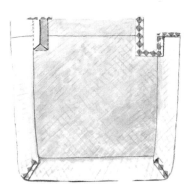

spaced **boxed pleats**

Box pleats need not meet fold to fold. When spaced apart, they make a short skirt look jaunty. To begin, determine the desired size of the face of the box pleat and of the space between box pleats. Then determine the amount to be folded at each side of each box pleat, which will add fullness.

For the pleated skirt on the chair shown, the face of the box pleat is 3", the space showing between pleats is 2", and 2" is folded at each side of each pleat (refer to Basics for more about pleats).

TIPS FROM THE PROS

✄A pleat is like a tuck that is creased and folded to one side. A box pleat is really a pair of pleats folded toward one another behind the face of the pleat.

✄To plan the pleat repeat, add together the size of the box pleat face and the pleat space. Check to see if the sum divides evenly into the length of the edge to which you will attach the skirt; adjust if necessary or plan to center a box pleat (or space) on the edge and let the ends fall as they will.

✄You may not know how you'll want to center the pleats until you pin the skirt to your project. So pleat more than you actually need, then cut it to size after aligning it properly.

1 Sew the pieces of the skirt together to form one length. Finish the seam allowances and hem the bottom edge.

2 Place the skirt right side up on your worktable. Starting several inches from one end, mark lines indicating each side of each box pleat face (A) and adjacent pleat space (B), allowing for a pleat of the desired size between each (A–B). ▽

3 Pleat the skirt, creasing the fabric on a pleat line (A) and folding it over to meet the line marking the adjacent space (B), pin. Repeat this across the skirt, alternating the direction of the folds. Baste across the top of the pleats. ▽

4 If you wish, sew across the top of the pleats to secure them. You can press the pleats flat, creasing all the folds sharply, or leave them soft.

This is a great design for dining chairs, which turn their backs on the room.

part three

basics

YOU'LL WANT TO GET OFF TO A CONFIDENT START NO

matter which slipcover you are making. While each

piece of furniture is unique and each slipcover

design has its own fitting and sewing requirements,

the basic construction process is similar for all.

In this section you'll find general directions for

calculating yardage, cutting, planning pattern

match, fitting, and basic sewing techniques. You'll

also find a list of the equipment and supplies

you're likely to need. Whether you are a novice

or experienced slipcover maker, review this

information, as it supports and enhances the

individual project directions.

calculating yardage

Novice slipcover makers are almost always intimidated by the thought of having to figure out how much fabric they'll need. There is no need to dread this task, as long as you plan your project thoroughly.

BEGIN WITH AN ESTIMATE
Having an approximate idea of the amount of fabric needed will help you plan the cost of your project. You can use the chart on the next page to quickly make an estimate.

First decide which item of furniture, below, your piece most closely resembles. Detailed directions for measuring your furniture and making a cutting layout from which to calculate the yardage appear later.

PLAIN FABRIC YARDAGE ESTIMATE CHART

		No Skirt	Standard Kick Pleat
A	Round Ottoman (up to 33" diameter)	$1^{1}/_{4}$	$2^{1}/_{2}$
B	Standard Ottoman (up to 23" x 23")	$1^{3}/_{4}$	$2^{3}/_{4}$
C	Large Ottoman (up to 27" x 27")	$2^{3}/_{4}$	$3^{3}/_{4}$
D	Dining Room Chair	$2^{1}/_{4}$	2
E	Armless Boudoir Chair	6	$7^{1}/_{2}$
F	Boudoir Armchair	$8^{1}/_{2}$	$10^{1}/_{2}$
G	Barrelback Chair	8	9
H	Fully Upholstered Armchair with Tight Back	8	9
I	Armchair with Removable Back Cushion	11	12
J	Wing Chair with Removable Deck Cushion	11	12
K	Chaise Lounge with Tight Seat and One Arm	15	17
L	Chaise Lounge with Removable Deck Cushion	14	$15^{1}/_{2}$
M	2-Cushion Loveseat with Tight Back (to 72" wide)	14	16
N	2-Cushion Sofa with Tight Back (up to 91" wide)	17	19
O	1-Cushion Camelback Sofa (up to 86" wide)	14	16
P	3-Cushion Sofa (up to 86" wide)	17	19
Q	2-Cushion Sofa with 2 Removable Back Cushions (up to 86" wide)	21	24
R	3-Cushion Sofa with 3 Removable Back Cushions (up to 86" wide)	21	24

The yardages listed above are for 54"-wide plain fabric placed vertically on the furniture (with the selvages perpendicular to the floor).

✂ For gathered and box-pleated skirt options, add the following additional yardage to standard kick-pleat skirt yardage

    ottoman/chair—1 yard

    chaise/loveseat—3 yards

    sofa—4 yards

✂ For contrasting welting, add the following additional yardage

    ottoman—1 yard

    chair—$1^{1}/_{2}$ yards

    chaise—2 yards

    loveseat—$2^{1}/_{2}$ yards

    sofa—3 yards

✂ Railroading fabric (placing it on the turniture with the selvages parallel to the floor) saves approximately 10% of the yardage

✂ The following yardage may be deducted when using a different deck fabric

    chair—1 yard

    chaise—2 yards

    loveseat—2 yards

    sofa—3 yards

TIPS FROM THE PROS

✂ The lengthwise grain of the fabric can be placed on the furniture perpendicular to the floor (vertically run) or parallel to it (railroaded). Although railroading the fabric requires a smaller amount of yardage, it is a good option only if your fabric looks well turned on its side. Some home decorating fabrics feature crosswise stripes. These are designed to be railroaded and make it possible to seamlessly place vertical stripes on a wide piece of furniture. Napped fabrics or those with patterns such as bouquets are not suitable for railroading. On the other hand, stripes can be very effective turned sideways. ▷

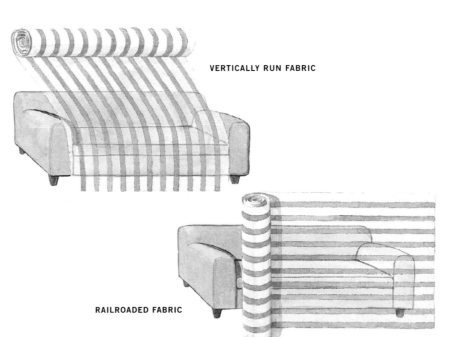

VERTICALLY RUN FABRIC

RAILROADED FABRIC

calculating yardage

Fabric Width	Plain Fabric	3"–14" Repeat	15"–19" Repeat	20"–27" Repeat	28"–36" Repeat	37"–45" Repeat	46"–54" Repeat
54"	0%	10%	15%	20%	25%	30%	35%
50"–52"	10%	20%	25%	30%	35%	40%	45%
48"	15%	25%	30%	35%	40%	45%	50%
45"	20%	30%	35%	40%	45%	50%	55%
36"	50%	60%	65%	70%	75%	80%	90%

Considering the Fabric Repeat

Fabrics with a repeating pattern usually require additional fabric. To determine a fabric's vertical repeat, find a dominant feature of the motif (the tip of a leaf, for instance) and mark it with a pin on two consecutive vertical motifs. Measure the distance between the pins. Determine the horizontal repeat in the same manner. Refer to page 106 for information on planning pattern match.

Once you have estimated the yardage you'd need if using plain fabric, you can use the chart above to estimate the requirements for a fabric with a repeating pattern. To use this chart, first add the fabric's vertical and horizontal repeats together (for example, a 10" vertical repeat plus a 17" horizontal repeat gives a 27" total repeat). Then find the appropriate entry on the chart, and increase the plain fabric estimate by the percentage indicated.

HOW TO MEASURE

Measuring the furniture is an essential step in making a slipcover. It begins the process of thinking about the number and shapes of the pattern pieces, which not only helps to determine the amount of fabric needed, but also gets you to think about how your slipcover will be put together. If you are designing your own slipcover, first make a sketch that indicates the principal seams. You don't have to be an artist—take photos of each view and sketch on tracing paper placed over them. If you are making one of the projects in this book, refer to the measuring diagrams given with the directions. If you wish to drape a muslin mock-up, measure first, then shape each piece following the general directions for pin fitting, page 109, as well as those given in the project directions. Later you can use the muslin as a pattern.

Seaming to Add Width

In addition to shaping the fabric pieces and giving style to a design, seams are used when one width of fabric is insufficient to span a section of the furniture—for instance, across the back of a sofa. Marking these seamlines on your furniture is optional, as you can measure the section and place the seams mathematically, but you might find it helpful to have the visual guide.

That being said, when you must piece fabric to obtain a greater width, do take the time to plan where the seams will fall. Avoid placing a vertical seam up the center of a sofa. Instead, use three panels of fabric, placing one in the center. If there are three cushions on the seat, you might want the piecing seams to align with the cushion junctions. Often, the center panel is wider than those on each side, which should be of equal width. Be sure the center panel is the same width on the seat, inside back, and outside back so the seams will align.

Determining Where You Want the Seams to Go

Before you can measure, you must establish the seam placement on your furniture. If you wish your slipcover to duplicate the general styling of your furniture's upholstery, the existing seamlines of the upholstery dictate the slipcover's seams. But if you want your slipcover to be a different style, or if you are covering a nonupholstered piece, you'll need to establish new seamlines. To do this, use dressmaker's chalk and simply draw new lines on the furniture or pin twill tape to the upholstery. If the furniture can't be pinned into, use a type of masking tape, such as drafting tape, that is easy to remove.

The thicker the back and arms of your furniture, the more dimension you need to build into your slipcover to be sure it fits over them. Slipcovers for nonupholstered chairs and benches require minimal dimension; those for upholstered pieces need more. Most commonly, you'll need to add dimension to the sides and top of a back, the top and front of an arm, and the sides of a seat or cushion. You do so by adding a strip of fabric (called boxing) between two pieces, or by shaping a flat piece with tucks, darts, or gathers when pin fitting (refer to pages 109–112). If you plan to add boxing, mark its seamlines on your furntiture.

TIPS FROM THE PROS

✂ Boxing strips give a more geometric, rigid, and even formal look to a piece of furniture and are especially useful when covering thicknesses greater than 3". Additionally, welting or other trim can be inserted in the boxing seams, adding strength and, if you like, color.

Naming the Pieces

Become familiar with the terminology used for slipcover pieces. The primary sections of a chair or sofa are: the outside back, the inside back, the seat (when there is not a separate seat cushion) or deck (under a separate seat cushion), the inside arm, the side (sometimes called the outside arm), the arm front, and the seat front. Slipcovers may also have a skirt, and it is not uncommon for this to be attached to a band that rings the furniture below

the seat. Sometimes a seat cover will extend over the edges of the seat. This extension, called a drop, can be hemmed or finished with a skirt. Covers for some types of furniture also have an outside wing and an inside wing, while others require a side back panel. Dimension is added to some slipcovers with a boxing strip placed along the top of the back or arms. Seat and back cushions have a cushion top and cushion bottom, which are joined by a boxing strip or band. ▽

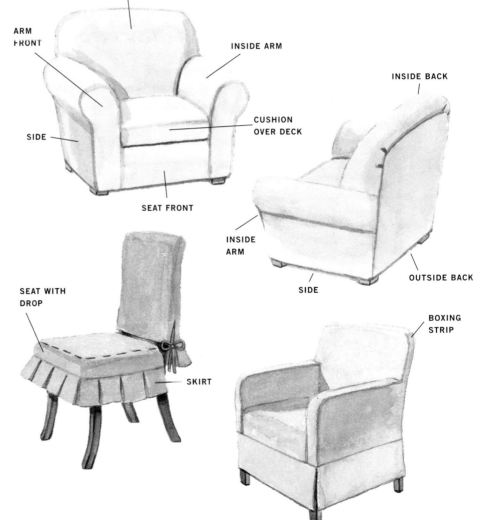

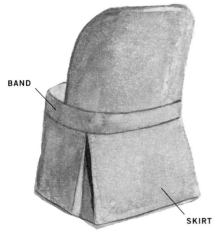

calculating yardage

Measuring

I D	Piece	Length x Width	Cutting Dimensions	Cut
A	Inside Back	25 x 25	33 x 33	1
B	Deck	20 x 20	28 x 24	1
C	Inside Arm	27 x 20	31 x 24	2
D	Side	12 x 24	16 x 28	2
E	Arm Front	23 x 10	27 x 14	2
F	Front	12 x 20	16 x 24	1

Once the seamlines are marked, make a chart that identifies each piece by name; it is also helpful to assign a letter ID to each as we have done in the project directions. Make a column in which to record the length and width of each piece, one for the cutting dimensions, and one in which to note the number needed of each. On the furniture, measure each piece between the marked seamlines, measuring at the widest and deepest points, and record the measurements in the Length & Width column on the chart. Measure the circumference for skirts and bands. If your design calls for two pieces to encase a chair back, be sure to include the thickness of the back in the length and width measurements. It is not necessary to record all the ins and outs of nonrectangular pieces; you'll establish their shapes during pin fitting. Prepare a paper label for each piece so that you'll be able to identify it once cut. Later, you'll use this chart to work out a cutting layout. △

In this book, the directions for each project include one or more measuring diagrams. The solid outlines indicate seams that fall over the upholstery seams or on logical edges of the furniture; the dash lines indicate seams that have been added to create the slipcover design, for instance, the line at which to attach or hem a skirt. The pairs of arrows on each section indicate where to measure; the letter identifies the piece and is repeated in the cutting list, cutting layout, and directions. If you are designing your own slipcover, you might find it helpful to create a similar diagram that is appropriate to your design. ▽

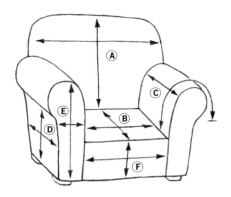

Adding Seam, Hem, and Tuck-in Allowances

Ease and seam, hem, and tuck-in allowances must be added to the piece measurements, and the fullness of gathered or pleated skirts can be figured from them. If your slipcover has only a few simply shaped pieces, you can probably add the seam and hem allowances to the measurements and use the totals to cut your pieces. However, many slipcovers require complex shaping that is easier to establish in the pin-fitting stage. If this is your situation, add 4"–8" to each measurement; this will ensure that you have enough fabric to adjust the ease and seams when you pin-fit. You can mark and trim the exact allowances afterward. Add the allowances to the dimensions on your chart, placing the totals in the Cutting Dimensions column.

The standard seam allowance for slipcovers is $1/2$". This should be added to each edge that will be sewn to another; it should also be used for welting flange allowance. Hem allowances can vary, depending upon the location of the hem, the weight of the fabric, and the style of the project. Hem allowance must be added at the bottom edge of the slipcover—which could be on the principal outside pieces, the drop, or attached skirts, depending on the design—and at vertical openings, such as side slits, which could include ruffle or skirt ends. Hem allowance must also be added to one end of cushion boxing strips (for a zipper tab overlap), to the bottom of inserted ruffles, and to the top and bottom of ruffles applied with a header.

Depending upon the fabric, the top edge of the hem can be finished by turning under or with a zigzag or serged stitch. Decide which method you'll use, and calculate the hem depth accordingly. The finished hem depth in lightweight fabrics is usually $^1/_2$"; in medium weight fabrics, 1"; in heavy fabrics, at least $1^1/_2$".

A tuck-in is the extra fabric that gets pushed down and tucked into furniture joints, such as where the deck meets the arms and inside back. Tuck-ins relieve stress from a sitter's weight and extend the life of the slipcover. When preparing a fabric piece that will tuck in, add 2" plus $^1/_2$" seam allowance. Sometimes you may also want to add a tuck-in to the inside arm/inside back seam; it should taper into the seam below the top of the arm, so shape it during pin fitting (refer to page 110).

Calculating Skirt and Ruffle Fullness

How full should a gathered skirt or ruffle be? This depends upon the desired effect and the weight of the fabric. Generally, the lighter the fabric, the greater the fullness. To determine the width of fabric needed, measure the circumference of the furniture or the width of the section to which the skirt or ruffle will be attached.
✂For lightweight fabrics, multiply the circumference or width by 3.
✂For heavier fabrics, multiply the circumference or width by $2^1/_2$.
✂Divide the total by the width of the fabric to establish the number of widths to cut. If the figure is a fraction, increase to the next whole number.

Don't forget that you'll lose 1" from each width for seam allowance. You'll also lose hem allowance if the ruffle is open on its ends.

TIPS FROM THE PROS
✂The only way you can be sure of the most effective ruffle fullness is to make a sample in your fabric. Cut ruffles generously and check their effect on the assembled slipcover; adjust as necessary.

Calculating Pleat Depth

Where a ruffle is inappropriate to the slipcover design, you can add fullness to a skirt by folding extra fabric smoothly to one side behind the face of the skirt. The distance from the outside vertical fold to the inside vertical fold is called the pleat depth. To determine the width of fabric needed for a pleated skirt, measure the circumference of the furniture or the width of the section that will have the skirt attached. ▽

PLEAT DEPTH

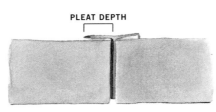

TWO PLEATS

✂Add twice the desired pleat depth for each pleat you plan to include.
✂Divide the total by the width of the fabric to establish the number of widths to cut. If the figure is a fraction, increase to the next whole number. Don't forget that you'll lose 1" from each width for seam allowance. You'll also lose hem allowance if the skirt is open on its ends.

TIPS FROM THE PROS
✂Plan the width of each panel of a pleated skirt so the seams will fall on the inside vertical fold of a pleat. If you make a diagram, you'll find it easier to plot this.

MAKING A SCHEMATIC DRAWING

To keep track of how much allowance to add to each edge of each piece of your slipcover, make a schematic drawing that shows all the pieces; draw allowances around each piece and note the depth of each. If you'll be establishing the final piece dimensions by pin fitting, draw a second allowance 2"–4" outside the measurement outlines for the pin-fitting allowance. ▽

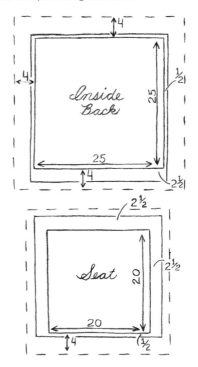

TIPS FROM THE PROS
✂If you make your schematic drawing to scale on graph paper, you can use it to work out your cutting layout later.

calculating yardage

MAKING A PAPER PATTERN

In slipcover making there is very little need for paper patterns, as the bulk of your cutting will be the slightly oversize rectangles that you pin-fit on your furniture. However, there are times when you may find it useful to work out a shape or detail on paper. (You can also use muslin for this. It can be pinned to the project, but it is not as easy to draw on.)

✀ Paper laid over a flat area, such as a dining chair seat or back, can be creased along the edge, or a shaped outline can be traced with a soft lead pencil.

✀ The scale and proportion of design details can be worked out on paper before committing to fabric. The number and shape of scallops on a border, the shape of an arm front, the depth of an inverted pleat, the proportion of a bottom band or bias binding can be worked out in full-size patterns or scale drawings.

If you wish to make multiples of a slipcover—as for a set of matching chairs—do make paper patterns from your pin-fit cover. Mark all the seamlines and seam allowances, trim the excess fabric, and disassemble the pieces. Then trace around each on a large piece of paper and cut out.

TIPS FROM THE PROS

✀ Use a dressmaker's needlepoint tracing wheel to transfer marks from muslin or pin-fit samples to paper.

MAKING A GRAPH PAPER LAYOUT

It is easier to calculate the total yardage needed for a piece of furniture if you draw a cutting layout. On a sheet of graph paper, establish a working scale. For example, decide that each square on the graph paper represents 4" of fabric. Using the length and width measurements recorded on your chart (including allowances), draw the basic rectangle for each piece you will be cutting. Label each and mark its top edge. Cut out each piece. On a larger piece of graph paper and using the same scale, draw two parallel lines to indicate the width of your fabric. On this arrange the cut-out pieces in an organized manner, using the least amount of fabric. Allow additional space for cutting bias strips (refer to page 108) or other details, such as bows and ties. ▽

✀ For vertically run fabric (with the selvage perpendicular to the floor) place the top of each cut-out piece toward one end of your fabric graph.

✀ For railroaded fabric (with the selvage parallel to the floor) place the top of each cut-out piece toward one side of your fabric graph.

✀ To enhance a slipcover design (to take advantage of a stripe, for instance) you might wish to cut some pieces on the crosswise or bias grain. If so, indicate this on the cutouts and place them in the appropriate orientation on the fabric graph.

✀ Bows and ties often behave best when their length is placed on the lengthwise grain.

✀ If there is no reason to cut pieces on different grainlines, avoid doing so. Instead, place the top edge of each in the same orientation.

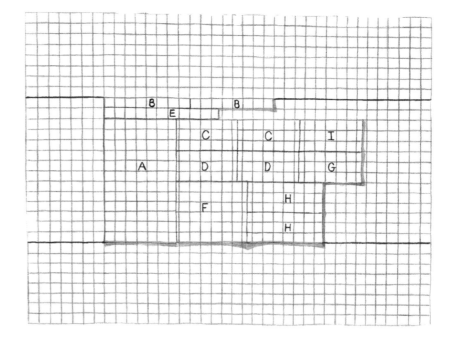

Along one long edge of your fabric graph, count the number of squares used in the arrangement. Multiply this by the assigned number of inches per square to calculate the total number of inches needed; divide this figure by 36 to find the required yardage. For instance, if your layout covers a length of 90 squares on the fabric graph and the scale is 4" per square, multiply 90 by 4 to see that you'll need 360" of fabric, or 10 yards.

When working with a fabric that has stripes or motifs to center or match, draw marks at the appropriate interval on the fabric graph to indicate the center of the pattern repeat. Also mark each cut-out paper rectangle with a line, X, or dot where you intend to position the center of the motif. When placing the cut-out pieces on the fabric graph, match the stripe or motif center markings. Refer to page 106 for information on how to match patterns. ▽

TIPS FROM THE PROS

✂Use transparent graph paper if your fabric has motifs to match, or mark the motif center on the "fabric" paper with dark pen that reads through the cut-out pieces.

✂Don't worry about matching the grid on your paper cutouts to that on the fabric graph—just keep the edges of the cut-outs parallel to the edges of the graph.

✂If cutting skirts, ruffles, or binding on the bias, remember to match stripes, checks, or plaids.

✂When matching a pattern, don't forget you'll need seam allowance on each side—if you just cut through the middle of a motif, you won't be able to sew it back together.

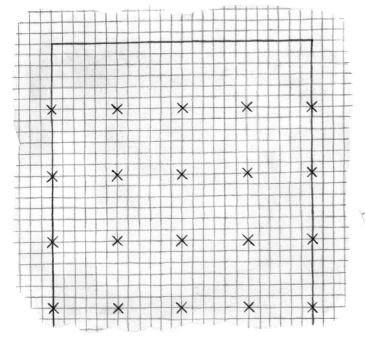

cutting a slipcover

For most slipcovers, once you have done your measuring and made a cutting layout, your next steps will be to shrink and press your fabric, cut out the slipcover pieces, and fit them on your furniture. However, if your fabric requires precise matching, first read Planning Pattern Match, below. If you wish to fit a mock-up before cutting the final cover, read Pin Fitting, pages 109–112, first.

PRESHRINKING

The type of fabric and use of the slipcover determine the type of cleaning your slipcover needs. If the fabric is a heavy upholstery-weight that is being used as a durable alternative to the original upholstery, then consider dry cleaning. If the slipcover is a lightweight fabric, then laundering may be the answer. However, certain colors may fade or bleed more than others, and some textures might change. Cleaning will generally remove finishes such as sizing and glazing. But many fabrics are not altered at all by cleaning. The important thing to remember is that testing is critical. If your test proves the washability of your fabric, then be sure to launder it before cutting to eliminate shrinkage of the finished slipcover.

It is always wise to test a fabric for shrinkage before cutting. Buy about ¹/₂ yard of fabric. Measure the length and width before laundering or dry cleaning. Remeasure after the cleaning process and determine the degree of shrinkage before you commit to purchasing the total amount of yardage.

PRESSING

Steam pressing the fabric before cutting not only aids in preshrinking but also results in a smooth, flat piece of fabric, ensuring accurate layout and cutting. If possible, to keep your fabric smooth roll it onto a long cardboard tube as you press.

TIPS FROM THE PROS

✄ To more easily press large areas, turn your ironing board 180 degrees so the square end is to your left. You can rest your iron on the narrow end and press on the larger surface.

✄ Sometimes the selvages are woven tighter than the rest of the fabric. If this is the case, cut them off, or snip them at regular intervals so the fabric will roll up smoothly and lie flat when you are ready to mark it.

PLANNING PATTERN MATCH

If your fabric has an obvious motif or pattern, experiment with the placement of the motifs on the piece of furniture before cutting. Center large motifs (including dominant stripes) on each section, or balance the visual weight of allover patterns. Then match the motifs as you pin-fit (refer to pages 109–112). Look through the photos in Part Two to see examples of pattern matching.

✄ Place the motifs on the inside back first. Then match them vertically from the inside back to the seat to the seat front to the skirt.

✄ If the slipcover has a seat cushion, match the top of the cushion to the inside back, and continue to match downward.

✄ Match the outside back to the inside back, keeping the same top orientation and aligning the motifs vertically and horizontally.

✄ Match the sides and/or outside arms to the back, aligning the motifs horizontally.

✄ Match the inside arms to the outside arms, keeping the same top orientation and aligning the motifs vertically and horizontally.

✄ In some instances, particularly on wing chairs, try to match the inside arms horizontally to the inside back.

To avoid miscuts on the final fabric, many people match by pin fitting muslin onto which the center or outline of each motif has been marked. An even easier way to plan pattern matches is to pin-fit using a sheer pattern tracing cloth onto which you have traced the general outlines of the motifs. (This cloth is similar to lightweight nonwoven interfacing and is printed with dots or lines in a 1" grid; it is available at notions and fabric stores.)

✄ Pin-fit the marked tracing cloth or muslin to your furniture, matching the motifs.

✄ Remove from the furniture, mark the seam allowances with a soft lead pencil, and trim the excess fabric.

✄ Place the tracing cloth patterns over your fabric and match the traced motifs to the woven or printed ones.

Placing Large Motifs

If your fabric has a large motif, it is probably more important to center the motif on each piece of the slipcover than it is to align or match it to adjacent sections. If you are unsure of which approach is better, consider how the slipcover will look when viewed from the side and the back, as well as from the front. For instance, if you center a motif on the inside back, above a seat cushion, and align a motif on the outside back at the same distance from the floor, the motif on the outside back is likely to be too high—the outside back would probably look better if the motif were centered.

However, if you are using a pattern with a strong horizontal line, such as a check or stripe placed parallel to the floor, do align it around the furniture. Plaids are the most difficult of all patterns to position, because they will not align where curves and angles on adjacent sections differ—on wings, scrolls, or even where a side meets a sloping back.

SETTING UP A WORKTABLE

If at all possible, set up a table on which to lay out and cut your slipcover. Ideally, to save wear on your back, it should be at hip height. You can use a 4' x 8' sheet of plywood set on sawhorses. Wrap the plywood with heavy paper or muslin to keep it from snagging your fabric, or better still, top it with $1/2$"-thick fiberboard (available at lumberyards), which is smooth and can be pinned into.

MARKING AND CUTTING

It is important to determine the right and wrong side of the fabric, or at least to be consistent in your choice. The right side is not always obvious. Generally, manufacturers roll fabrics on the bolt with the right side to the inside. Selvages may have woven words or printed symbols and other information on the right side. Otherwise, identifying the right side is sometimes simply a matter of preference.

If the wrong side is not obvious, identify it on the the selvage at intervals when you lay your fabric on your cutting table—use a pencil, safety pin, or tape—and mark each piece as it is cut. Likewise, if working with a napped fabric, draw an arrow indicating the direction in which the nap should lie— and make a note to remind yourself whether the arrow is to point up or down when you assemble the pieces.

If you consistently mark the wrong side of the fabric, you won't have to worry about removing the marks later. If possible, lay your fabric out wrong side up so you can mark all cutting lines and match points on the wrong side. However, to accurately match a pattern that shows only on the right side, you'll have to lay the fabric out right side up.

Refer to your schematic drawing and layout (pages 103 and 104) as you mark the fabric—these show you the dimensions of each piece, as well as the amount of seam allowance to include for the pin-fitting stage. If your cover has irregularly shaped pieces, don't worry about marking them out perfectly; include extra seam allowance and trim it when you are fitting the cover on your furniture. (If you have made a mock-up and are using it as a pattern, you won't need extra seam allowance.) The layout also shows the orientation of each piece, reminding you to place all the hem edges toward the selvage (for railroaded fabric) or end (for vertically run fabric).

As you mark, be sure each piece lies squarely on the fabric; The lengthwise grain is parallel to the selvage; measure two points equidistant from one edge to find it. The crosswise grain is perpendicular to the selvage; use a square or 90-degree triangle to find it. For pieces that are not perfectly square or rectangular, the vertical center of each should be perpendicular to the floor; place it on the straight grain. ▽

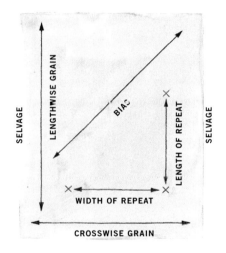

To be sure you have enough fabric you should mark out all the pieces before cutting any. The marked fabric should look like your cutting layout. It is not necessary to mark all the bias strips for welting, just mark an area to set aside for them. If your project has a skirt, you might want to cut, pin-fit, and sew the body before cutting the skirt itself— should you decide to change the proportions of the body, you'll be able to easily adjust the skirt to match.

As the various fabric pieces are cut, pin labels that correspond to your chart to each piece.

cutting a **slipcover**

ABOUT BIAS STRIPS

Because it stretches, is flexible, and curves nicely, true bias, which falls on a 45-degree angle between the lengthwise and crosswise grainlines, should be used to cover welting or bind project edges. When planning to use bias for welting or binding, purchase at least an additional $1/2$ yard of fabric. The more extra fabric you buy, the longer each bias strip will be, the fewer seams you'll need to join them, and the smoother the finished trim will be.

One-half yard of fabric yields 11 to 13 yards of bias, and 1 yard will give 22 to 26 yards. How much will you need? A wing chair can easily require between 15 and 20 yards of welting.

Bias strips can be used as a single layer or folded in half lengthwise and sewn through both layers (called double, or French fold, bias). To determine the width to cut a bias strip, first calculate the width the strip should be when finished.

✄ For welting, the finished width is the amount needed to wrap around the cording; add twice the seam allowance to this dimension to find the cut width. If you wish to cover the cord with a double layer of fabric, double the second number.

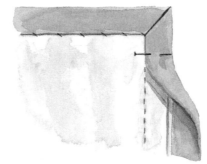

✄ For binding, the finished width is the amount of binding you wish to show on the right side along the edge of the project. Binding is easiest to apply when its seam allowance is equal to its finished width. For single binding, shown above, quadruple the finished width to find the cut width. For French fold binding, multiply the finished width by six to find the cut width. △

TIPS FROM THE PROS

✄ If binding heavy fabric or multiple layers, add about $1/8$" to the cut width of the binding so it will turn comfortably over the project edge.

Cutting Bias Strips

To find the bias, place one leg of a 45-degree triangle on the selvage and mark along the hypotenuse, or fold the fabric diagonally so the crosswise threads are parallel to the selvage and mark the fold. In slipcover making you will probably need a substantial quantity of bias; you can mark and cut the strips individually, but here is an efficient way to cut large quantities:

Mark the longest possible bias line on your fabric, and cut along it. Beginning at one 45-degree corner, fold the fabric repeatedly, aligning the bias edge. Mark strips of the desired width parallel to the bias edge, and cut through all layers—pin first to keep the layers aligned. Refold the fabric as needed. (If you use a rotary cutter and transparent ruler, you won't have to mark the strips or pin the layers.) ▽

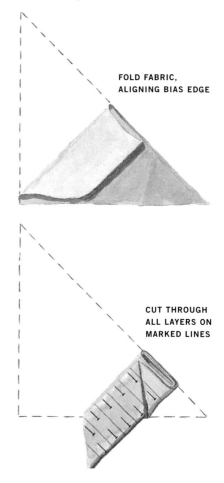

FOLD FABRIC, ALIGNING BIAS EDGE

CUT THROUGH ALL LAYERS ON MARKED LINES

Pin fitting the pieces of the slipcover directly on the furniture customizes its fit, allowing you to adjust proportions, add dimension to flat shapes, and fine-tune corners and intersections. The project directions in this book tell you the order in which to work. If possible, work with the fabric right side down on the furniture. This will make it easier to later mark the seamlines, allowances, and match points.

If your furniture is symmetrical and you are working with a plain fabric, a woven pattern, or a print on which the pattern shows through to the wrong side, you can pin-fit with the fabric wrong side up. If you are making a tight slipcover, be aware that the right and left sides of apparently symmetrical upholstered pieces may not be truly identical—when in doubt, pin-fit with the fabric right side up.

When working with an asymmetrical piece, such as a single-end chaise lounge or an ultramodern sofa or chair, or when working with a print fabric with no show-through, then it is necessary to pin-fit with the fabric right side up. Proceed with the pin fitting in the normal manner. When you are ready to sew, snip small notches or mark with tailor's chalk at regular intervals along the seam allowances. Remove the pins along one seam allowance length at a time, reposition the seam allowances to the inside, and repin, matching the notches or markings.

POSITIONING THE FABRIC

As you begin laying the fabric rectangles on the furniture, you may need to hold some pieces in place before you can actually begin to pin-fit. To do this, place T-pins at the corners of a section. When working on a wood- or metal-framed piece, hold the fabric in place with masking tape. Center each piece on the corresponding section of the furniture, and smooth outward in all directions.

In order to shape the pieces properly, you will probably have to trim some excess fabric as you pin-fit, especially at curved areas, such as where the top of the arm meets the inside back. Leave enough to make further adjustments. You may also have to slash or clip into the seam allowance in these areas to allow the fabric to change direction or lie flat. ▽

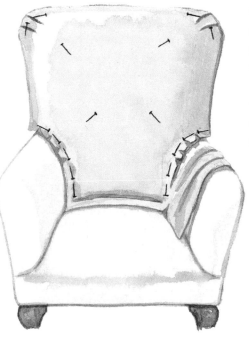

Pin the pieces together along the seamlines you established when measuring the furniture. Position the pins lengthwise along the seamlines so you can see exactly how the cover is fitting; adjust the seams as needed until you are pleased with the effect.

When three or more pieces come together, leave the seam allowance unpinned so it can spread or turn where the pieces meet. Later, when you sew the cover, stop sewing this seam at the intersecting seamline. △

TIPS FROM THE PROS
✂ Take your time fitting, and stand back to check that everything is hanging properly, with hems parallel to the floor. When you are satisfied with the final look and fit, trim the seam allowances to $1/2$".

pin fitting

✄When making a simple slipcover, you may be able to go directly from pin fitting to sewing. Check that all the pins are on the same side of the project, either on the seamline with their heads facing toward you, so you can pull them out as they reach the needle, or perpendicular to the seamline with their heads toward the cut edges, so you can sew across them.

TUCK-INS

While pin fitting, include tuck-ins along the adjacent edges of the seat or deck and inside arms and inside back. If your slipcover sits over a separate cushion, the tuck-in fits between the cushion and the inside arms and inside back. It is customary to allow a tuck-in even when the slipcover deck will be covered by a cushion—the allowance just folds onto the deck or tucks into the crevice between the deck and the inside arms and inside back. Likewise, you should allow a tuck-in when slipcovering furniture with tight upholstery (no removable cushions); the allowance gets tucked into the crevice between the seat and the arms and inside back. Sometimes you may also want to add a tuck-in to the inside arm/inside back seam; this should be tapered into the top of the seam.
✄For tuck-ins, allow about 2" on each piece, plus the $^{1}/_{2}$" seam allowance.
✄Do not try to pin the front ends of the seat tuck-in to another piece of the cover. Leave them free so the tuck-in can turn or fold as needed. ▷

TIPS FROM THE PROS

✄Later, when you sew the cover together, remember to sew the tuck-ins $^{1}/_{2}$" from their cut edges, as shown by the yellow lines in the drawing below, not along the pin-fitting lines.
✄Keep the front ends of the tuck-ins free as pinned when you sew the front band or skirt to the seat and arm front. Stop the seam at the intersection of the arm front/inside arm seam and start again on the other side of the seat tuck-in, as shown by the breaks in the yellow lines in the drawing below.
✄If you find tuck-ins difficult to understand, examine some display samples in a furnishings store to see how they work.
✄When the slipcover is finished and on the furniture, insert the tuck-ins, then place a foam wedge or cardboard tube in each to keep it in place.

SLASHING TO FIT

Slash a flat piece of fabric to spread the seam allowance over or around an intersecting plane on the furniture; for instance, where an arm rail meets the inside back or an arm post meets the seat. Slash only up to the seamline and make only as many cuts as are needed. Before making any slashes, be sure your fabric is properly centered on the furniture; smooth it out evenly in all directions, getting it to lie as flat as possible before you have to slash. You may find it helpful to first trim some of the excess fabric.

When ready to slash, cut from the outside edge of the fabric toward the seamline.
✄When shaping a curved seamline, slash at intervals. After each slash, smooth the fabric against the furniture to establish the next part of the curve, then slash again.

✂When shaping an angular opening around a post or rail, use a Y-slash. First slash from the fabric edge toward the center of the post, then slash diagonally into each corner. △
✂When shaping an inside corner, slash diagonally right into the corner.

TIPS FROM THE PROS

✂When possible, fold the excess fabric back onto the furniture so you can judge where to end the slash. This allows you a good view of the intersecting plane and lessens the danger of inadvertently snipping your furniture.

✂Reinforce slashes by staystitching along the seamline. Add a small piece of interfacing to areas that take stress.

SHAPING AND EASING EXCESS FABRIC

Use the following techniques to ease fullness at a curve, such as on the shoulders or scroll arms of an upholstered chair, or to form a corner in a flat piece of fabric so it will accommodate the thickness of a cushion or nonupholstered chair frame.

Gathers

Pin together the two pieces of fabric along the seamline up to the curved area. Work running stitches by hand along the seamline of the piece to be eased. To adjust the fullness pull the needle, sliding the fabric toward the thread knot until it fits against the other layer of fabric. Secure the thread with a few stitches or by wrapping in a figure eight around a pin. The fullness will be permanently eased when you sew the two layers of fabric together. ▽

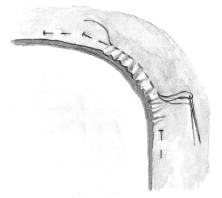

For especially even gathers, relax the hand gathers and, following their line, gather again by machine before sewing the final seam.

Darts

Pin together the two pieces of fabric along the seamline up to the curved area. Align the midpoint of the larger piece with the midpoint of the smaller one. Working outward from the midpoint, pinch and pin the excess fabric into tapered darts so the larger piece fits against the smaller one. Pin or hand-baste securely along the length of each dart.

When you remove the cover from the furniture, sew each dart individually by machine, and press all in one direction before sewing the seam joining the two pieces of fabric. ▽

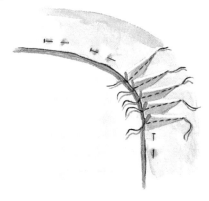

If you want to make an informal slipcover that looks as though it is just a large piece of fabric draped over the furniture, you can use darts to give it some shape and keep it under control. Place the fabric over the furniture and experiment to find attractive ways to dart out some of the excess volume. The cover on pages 48–49 was made in this manner.

Tucks

Pin together the two pieces of fabric along the seamline up to the curved area. Align the midpoint of the larger piece with the midpoint of the smaller one. Starting at one end, pinch and pin the excess fabric into tucks so the larger piece fits against the smaller one. Fold the tucks in one direction, and pin or baste across the wide end. If the tucks will overlap, pin the lowest one first. The fullness will be permanently eased when you sew the two pieces of fabric together; the tucks will form soft, tapered pleats.

Note that tucks folded on the wrong side of the cover will face in the opposite direction when the fabric is turned right-side out; in our illustration they will face up on the finished slipcover. ▽

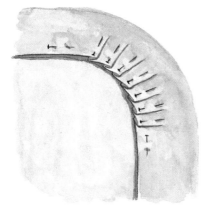

Dart Miters

Use dart miters to box a corner (as on a back or seat) without adding a separate strip of fabric. Position the fabric on the back or seat, smooth, and wrap over the edges. Pin toward each corner, where the excess fabric will form a diagonal fold. Pin along the corner and trim the excess fabric.

When you remove the cover from the furniture, sew the corner darts before joining the fabric to another piece; press the darts open. △

FITTING EXAGGERATED SHAPES

The tighter you make your slipcover, the more the pieces must conform to the shape of the furniture—and the more precise your work must be. However, for casual slipcovers, such strict conformity is not really necessary. For instance, if your furniture has scroll arms, you can shape the cover so it skims rather than hugs them. To do this, let the side of the cover hang straight from the top of arm to the floor, shaping the excess on the front of the arm with minimal tucks and making an arm front piece that does not conform exactly to the shape of the scroll it covers. If necessary, make the slipcover back wide enough to span the back of the arm, contouring the back gently from the top to the widest point.

If you wish, before sewing a cover that has been fitted this way, interface any portions that float loosely over furniture to prevent them from collapsing over the smaller shapes they mask.

construction techniques

You'll use a variety of sewing techniques as you make your slipcover. If you are an experienced sewer, you'll see that making a slipcover does not differ greatly from making apparel. Whatever your skill level, take the time to review the following information, as some techniques may be unfamiliar to you.

PRESSING

Pressing during each stage of construction will result in a good-looking slipcover that requires only a light touch-up when completed.

TIPS FROM THE PROS

✄ After sewing a seam, press the seam flat to meld the stitches and then, in most cases, press the seam allowance open. When seams fall on an edge of the furniture or have welting, press them down or away from the furniture.

✄ If seams are bulky and turned together in one direction, grade (trim) each layer to a different width. Generally, the seam allowance closest to the top fabric is left widest. Grading helps seams lie flat without bulk so they don't appear as unsightly ridges on the right side of your slipcover.

HAND-SEWING TECHNIQUES

Hand sewing is used for temporary stitching or for finishing. Use a single, rather than double, strand of thread and wax it for better control. For temporary stitching, do not knot the thread; secure it with a couple of small stitches instead. This assures that you'll cut the thread to free it before pulling it out—pulling forgotten knots through the fabric can leave holes or otherwise mar its surface.

Blindstitch

The blindstitch is used for hemming and holding facings in place, and is inconspicuous on both sides. First, finish the cut edge of the hem or facing. Roll this edge back about $1/4$". Work from right to left. Make a small horizontal stitch under one thread of the fabric, then under a thread of the hem or facing diagonally opposite the first stitch. ▽

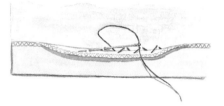

Catchstitch

The catchstitch holds two layers of fabric in place while allowing some flexibility in their alignment. Use it to attach raw or finished edges of facings and interfacings to the wrong side of fabrics; it is particularly useful when the layers will lie over a curved surface. Work from left to right but insert the needle from right to left. Make a small horizontal stitch in one layer, then make a second stitch diagonally opposite the first in the other layer. Repeat, alternating stitches along the edge in a zigzag fashion and keeping threads loose. ▽

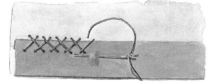

The blind catchstitch is good for hemming heavy fabrics. Finish the cut edge of the hem and roll the hem back about $1/4$". Make catchstitches between the two layers of fabric, keeping stitches loose.

Running Stitch

The running stitch is a temporary stitch used for basting seams to secure their alignment during construction and for gathering or easing during pin fitting. Space stitches evenly, $1/4$" long and $1/4$" apart. If basting to align a pattern, be precise, inserting the needle perpendicularly through all layers and checking as you work. ∨

Slipstitch

The slipstitch provides an almost invisible finish for hems, linings, and trims. Working from right to left, insert the needle into the folded edge of the upper layer, slide it inside the fold, bring it out about $1/8$"–$1/4$" from the insertion point, then slide the needle under a single thread of the lower layer. Repeat. When slipstitching braids or other trims, slide the needle through and along the woven or twisted edge, concealing the thread. ▽

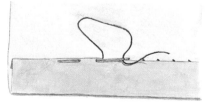

construction techniques

MACHINE-SEWING TECHNIQUES

The directions in this book call for a variety of machine stitches and seams. These are explained below, along with some others that you may find useful.

Baste

To sew with temporary stitches, either to hold pieces together so you can check the fit or to secure two layers to which a third will be added, as when inserting welting. Basting allows you to accurately align seams. Use the longest stitch setting. If you are matching pieces prior to making permanent seams, sew on the seamline. If you are holding multiple layers together so they can be treated as one, sew in the seam allowance.

Staystitch

To reinforce a seamline before sewing one piece of fabric to another, usually so that the seam allowance can be clipped and spread without risk of tearing. Generally, staystitching is done through one layer of fabric with a short straight stitch.

Edgestitch

To secure a folded edge to another layer of fabric by topstitching through all layers as close to the fold as possible.

Topstitch

To stitch through one or more layers with the project right side up in the machine. Topstitching can be decorative or functional or both. Use a thread color and stitch length that are appropriate to the situation.

Finish the Edge

For durability, the cut edge of seam allowances should not be left raw. In general, you should finish the edges as you work, selecting a method that is appropriate for your fabric and equipment—zigzag, serge, fold-and-topstitch are three common options. In this book, the direction to "finish the edges" is given as a reminder only when we felt it would be difficult to accomplish at a later stage.

Gather

To draw up a length of fabric with stitches, as when making a ruffle. Gathers can be adjustable, so you can manipulate and distribute the fullness as desired. If you have a ruffler foot or attachment, they can be stitched to a set tension; these will be even, but cannot be tightened or loosened, so refer to the attachment manual and make a test piece.

✄For basted adjustable gathers, make two parallel rows of basting stitches, one on the seamline, one just inside the seam allowance. Pull the bobbin threads to gather the fabric to the desired fullness; wrap them in a figure eight around a pin to secure temporarily. ▽

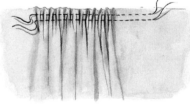

✄For zigzag adjustable gathers, lay button thread or monofilament over the seamline and zigzag stitch over it. Pull the button thread to gather the fabric to the desired fullness; wrap it in a figure eight around a pin to secure temporarily. ▽

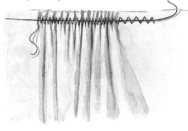

TIPS FROM THE PROS

✄When gathering long pieces, make several short runs of gathering stitches—they're easier to pull up without breaking. First divide the edge to be gathered into logical segments—for instance, quarter it to apportion to each side of a square seat or pillow.

✄If only a slight amount of easing is required, try this technique: Use a regular stitch length and with one finger pressing against the lower back of the presser foot, sew for about 2". Release your finger to allow the fabric to move out of the way, and repeat several times.

Serged Seam

A serger produces an overlocking stitch to prevent raveling as it trims excess fabric from the seam allowance. A three-thread stitch formation is commonly used as an edge finish. A four-thread stitch formation can seam and finish in one pass.

Zigzag Seam

A sturdy, ravel-proof seam. Place the fabric right sides together. Stitch on the seamline, using a narrow short zigzag 1mm wide and 1mm long. In the seam allowance, stitch again, using a zigzag 2mm wide and 2mm long. Trim the excess seam allowance.

Flat-Felled Seam

A sturdy, flat, enclosed seam that can be made on the right or wrong side of a project. Allow at least 5/8" seam allowance width when cutting. Sew a plain seam, and press it to one side. Trim the bottom seam allowance to 1/8". Turn under 1/4" on the edge of the top seam allowance and place back over the narrow seam allowance. Machine stitch close to the folded edge. ▽

French Seam

An enclosed seam well suited to straight seams on sheer fabric. Allow 5/8" seam allowance when cutting. With fabric wrong sides together, stitch a plain seam 3/8" from the seamline in the seam allowance. Trim to 1/8" from stitching. Press the seam to one side. Fold along the stitched seam, bringing the right sides of the fabric together, and press. Stitch along the seamline, encasing the raw edges. ▽

Rolled Hem

Rolled hems are narrow, softly rolled edges created with a special rolled hem attachment or adjustment on a serger, or with a special presser foot on a sewing machine. They are commonly used on sheers and lightweight fabrics. Make a test to determine the appropriate seam allowance and stitch length for your fabric.

TIPS FROM THE PROS

✄A quick rolled hem can be made on a lightweight or sheer fabric by folding the fabric to the wrong side and stitching with a narrow short zigzag stitch, 1mm wide and 1mm long, on the folded edge. On the wrong side, carefully trim the excess fabric close to the stitching.

Stitch-Turn-Stitch Baby Hem

A delicate, completely finished hem for sheers and lightweight fabrics. Stitch through one layer of fabric in the seam allowance 1/8" from the hemline. Press the fabric to the wrong side along the stitching line, then stitch close to the folded edge. On the wrong side, carefully trim the excess fabric close to the stitching. Press the fabric to the wrong side along this stitching line, and stitch again next to the new fold. ▽

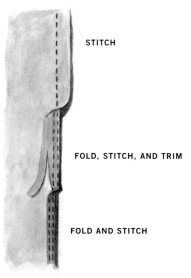

STITCH

FOLD, STITCH, AND TRIM

FOLD AND STITCH

construction techniques

SEWING CORNERS AND CURVES

When joining a straight edge to a corner or curve, you will have to clip the seam allowance of one piece or the other so the layers will lie flat while you sew the seam. You'll encounter this situation whenever you are sewing a boxing band to a cushion or below the seat of a chair or when an inside arm is sewn to a T-shaped inside back. If you have never sewn these seams, test the techniques using muslin or scraps of your fabric.

Outside Corners

To turn a corner when attaching a straight piece, such as a boxing band or welting, pin the band to the other piece of fabric above the corner, right sides together and cut edges aligned. At the corner, clip the seam allowance of the band only right up to the seamline, pivot the band around the corner, and continue pinning. ▽

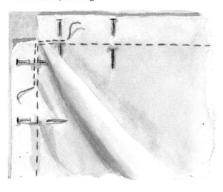

TIPS FROM THE PROS

✄If there is a seam in the straight piece where it meets the corner, don't clip, just remove the stitches from the end of the seam.

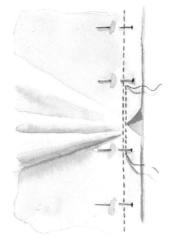

Inside Corners

To attach a straight piece, such as a boxing band or welting, to an inside corner, first staystitch the corner along the seamline and clip the corner seam allowance right up to the stitches. Pin the piece with the corner to the band, right sides together and cut edges aligned, spreading the fabric to fit the band. △

Outside Curves

To attach a straight piece, such as a boxing band or welting, to an outside curve, pin the straight piece to the curved piece, right sides together and cut edges aligned. At the curve, clip the seam allowance of the band only right up to the seamline, clipping only as needed to spread the seam allowance around the curve. ▽

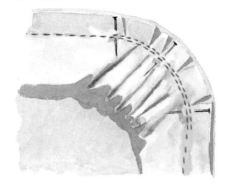

Inside Curves

To attach a straight piece, such as a boxing band or welting, to an inside curve, first staystitch the curved section along the seamline. Pin the piece with the curve to the band, right sides together and cut edges aligned. Clip the seam allowance of the curve right up to the staystitching, clipping only as needed to spread the fabric to fit the band. ▽

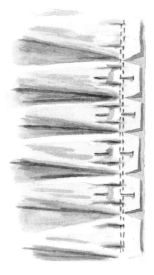

TIPS FROM THE PROS

✄Before clipping into a seam allowance, staystitch the seamline to reinforce it.

✄When attaching a straight band to a piece that has both inside and outside corners or curves, place pins on both sides of the seam. Hand-baste these sections before sewing so you won't have to pull pins out from the underside as they reach the needle.

✄When inserting welting between two pieces of a slipcover, sew it to the right side of one piece along the seamline before topping with the second piece.

HEMS

Hems can be made by hand or machine, as you wish, although in slipcover making, there is generally little reason to hem by hand. Because sewing equipment and fabric choice play a part in choosing the best hem method, the directions in this book do not always recommend a specific technique. Refer to page 102 for information about adding hem allowance. Refer to hand-sewing techniques, page 113, and machine-sewing techniques, page 114, for specific stitches.

USING BATTING

A slipcover flatlined with batting has a lush, quilted look. Batting will make a hard chair a bit more comfortable to sit on, but its primary purpose is to add substance to the cover and mask sharp edges or uneven surfaces such as rush seats or buttoned upholstery. Omit batting from hem allowances and ruffles. You can use packaged quilters' batting, which comes in several different thicknesses and densities, or buy it by the yard from a good notions vendor or upholstery supplier. Fusible fleece batting is also available.

Back each piece of batting with a matching piece of muslin or batiste. Baste the batting to the backing with long running stitches in a large grid. Place the wrong side of the slipcover fabric on the batting, and baste together along the seamlines; then treat as one layer when sewing your slipcover together. For best results, trim the batting from the seams to eliminate bulk.

USING TRIMS

Trims dress up a slipcover. Inserted in seams and placed along edges, they take more stress from everyday use than you might anticipate, so select varieties that appear durable. Whether you make or purchase your trims, preshrink them if appropriate.

Joining Bias Strips

Press-stretch bias strips before working with them for easier handling and smoother results. Before joining the strips, check to see that their ends are on the straight grain; recut if necessary. Place two strips right sides together, with the ends aligned as shown, and sew together. Repeat to join all the strips, then press all the seam allowances open. ▽

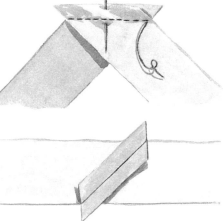

TIPS FROM THE PROS

✂ When piecing striped, napped, or otherwise directionally patterned bias strips, check to be sure that the pattern or nap is always facing the same way—you may have to recut the ends of the strips (to the opposite straight grain) to maintain the alignment.

Welting

To make welting, put a zipper or piping foot on your machine, aligning it to the left of the needle. Center cable cord on the wrong side of a bias strip. Fold the strip over the cord, aligning cut edges—there is no need to pin. Feed the cord and bias into the machine with the cord to the right of the needle, the seam allowance to the left under the foot. Stitch close to the cord, continuing to fold the bias over the cord as you sew. Trim the seam allowances to an even $1/2$". ▽

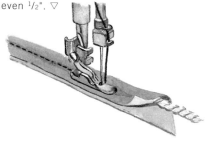

To attach welting, pin it to the right side of the slipcover section, aligning the cut edges. Position the zipper or piping foot to the right of your needle, and feed the piece into the machine, welting side up, with the cord to the left of the needle and the seam allowance to the right, under the foot. Stitch over the previous stitching on the welting. ▽

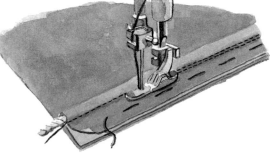

construction techniques

To attach another piece of fabric, such as a facing, boxing, or lining, place the two pieces right sides together, with the wrong side of the welted piece facing up. Align the cut edges and pin along the previous line of stitching. Move the needle position closer to the welting and stitch right next to the previous stitching.

To end welting at a seam or edge, stop stitching just before the intersecting seamline. Push the bias casing back and trim the inner cord. Pull the bias back over the cord, swing the folded edge of the welting across the seamline, and stitch over it. ▽

When welting ends must butt (as when rimming a cushion), place the join at the center of the least conspicuous edge, not at a corner. Leave both ends of the welting free for about 1". Remove the stitching that secures the bias over the cord from one end of the welting, and cut the cord so it butts the other end. Fold up the end of the extra bias and place the other end of the welting on it. Wrap the bias over the joint and complete the seam. ▽

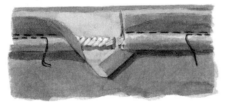

✄ Use French fold bias when working with sheer fabrics—it will be self-lined and mask the cord or fabric it covers.
✄ Welting made with French fold bias can double as trim *and* facing—make it so the flange with the folded edge extends the width desired for the facing.

Single and Double Binding

Binding encloses an edge without adding or subtracting dimension, so cut the edge you plan to bind on its finished line—trim any seam or hem allowance before applying the binding. The bias strips used for binding can be applied single or double.

When binding is applied double, it is sometimes called French fold binding. French fold binding is a good choice for lightweight fabrics. It is faster to apply because the edge that is turned to the inside of the project is already folded and ready to hem.

Applying Single Binding

1 Press the binding strip in half lengthwise, right side out. Unfold the binding and press the cut edges to the center creaseline. ▽

2 Unfold the binding on one edge. With right sides together and cut edges aligned, pin the binding to the edge of the project. Stitch along the creaseline. ▽

3 Fold the binding to the wrong side of the project, encasing the cut edge. On the wrong side, align the folded edge of the binding with the line of stitching. Pin and slipstitch. ▽

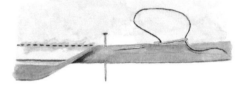

4 If the ends of the binding will be covered by an adjacent seam, leave them unfinished. If an end requires finishing, fold up the seam allowance before sewing the binding to the project. To join the ends of the binding, fold one end up and lap the other end over it, then sew through all layers. ▽

Applying Double Binding

1 Press the binding strip in half lengthwise, right side out.

2 With right sides together and cut edges aligned, pin the binding to the edge of the project. Stitch together, placing the seam one-third of the folded strip's width from the edge.

To complete the binding, follow steps 3 and 4 for Single Binding, opposite.

TIPS FROM THE PROS

✂ French fold binding can be machine stitched to the wrong side of the project when it has been cut slightly wider than needed. Apply and fold it over the edge in the usual manner; the folded edge of the binding will extend beyond the stitching line. Pin, and on the right side of the project, stitch in the ditch of the seam through all layers.

Purchased Trims

Purchased trims, such as decorator welting or piping, cord, braid, and fringe, add a professional touch to a slipcover. Many styles ravel when cut, and finishing their ends can be awkward. Use care and common sense when working with them, keeping the cut ends wrapped with tape until ready for the final finishing. Sew decorator welting to your project as you do fabric-covered welting (see page 117). Cord must be sewn on by hand. Braid and fringe can be sewn on by hand or machine, depending upon the type and the intended use. If possible, finish their ends by turning under or concealing in an adjacent seam. Otherwise, use a fray retardent or bind with small stitches.

To join the ends of twisted-cord piping, snip the stitches that hold the cord to the tape flange, freeing about $1^1/_2$" at each end. Overlap the ends of the tape, folding up the bottom one behind the top one. Wrap the cord ends together in consecutive order, overlapping them on the tape. Staystitch the cords to the tape. ▽

TIPS FROM THE PROS

✂ The terms *welting* and *piping* are used interchangeably by most people. They refer to round trim that has a flange (sometimes called a lip), which is sewn into the seams of the slipcover. Welting and piping can be fabric covered or made of decorative twisted cords.

✂ The terms *cord* or *cording* refer to a cord that has no flange or lip. Cable cord is the cord used inside fabric-covered welting.

✂ Fringe is held together with stitches along one edge. This area is called a header. Many professionals conceal the header behind a hem or tuck. However, some headers are attractive, and you can stitch them on top of your project if you like the effect.

✂ Some fringes and trims are heavy. Interface or line your project so it will support a heavy trim without puckering.

Ruffles

Ruffles can be cut on either the straight or bias grainline and there are a number of factors that influence your choice of which to use. In general, ruffles cut on the straight grain tend to be crisp, while those cut on the bias drape softly, but the hand of the fabric also influences this. Additionally, directional fabrics, such as stripes, checks, and plaids, have different effects when run vertically, horizontally, or diagonally. Bias-cut ruffles can stretch along the edges, so add trim to them carefully to avoid distortion; heavy trim may cause them to stretch from top to bottom. When a strip of fabric is made into a ruffle, gathers or pleats are secured a short distance from one edge. The area above the gathers is called a header.

✂ If the header edge is finished with a hem or trim, the ruffle is applied on top of whatever it is to adorn so the header adds a flourish; it can be any depth that seems pleasing. Applied ruffles can usually be topstitched to a project by machine, but dimensional trims used to cover the gathers may have to be sewn on by hand. ▽

✂If the header edge is left raw, the ruffle must be sewn on so that it extends from under the project edge. In this case, the header should be the depth of the seam allowance used throughout the project. When you are ready to attach the ruffle, pin it to the project with right sides together and cut edges aligned. Welting or other trim can be inserted between the ruffle and the project. ▽

If a ruffle will be open on its ends, hem the ends before hemming the top and bottom edges. If it will be closed, sew the joining seam before hemming the top and bottom edges. If you'll be adjusting the ruffle fullness in your fitting process, leave the end of the hem open and complete it after hemming or joining the perpendicular edge.

Skirts

Gathered or pleated skirts are just large ruffles. To attach them, follow the preceding directions. Because slipcover skirts are likely to be heavy or awkward to manipulate, be sure to gather them in small, logical segments to minimize the risk of thread breaks. Baste pleats by hand or machine before pinning to the slipcover, so you don't lose them if the pins fall out while you're working.

FASTENINGS

Loose-fitting slipcovers may slide right over your furniture, but, like clothing, those with a closer fit, those that cover curvy pieces, and cushion covers need openings that can be secured once the cover is in place.

Hook-and-Loop Tape

Suitable for securing lapped openings. Hook-and-loop tape (Velcro™) is available in coin shapes, small squares, small fastener strips, and by the yard in $^5/_8$", $^3/_4$", $1^1/_2$", and 2" widths. To apply, straight-stitch along each outer edge. The tape has no bias, so tends to stiffen seams. Avoid applying to seams that lie over a curved surface.

Slot Zipper

Install centered on a plain seam, as on the back boxing strip of a cushion. Sew the seam, basting the portion where the zipper will go, and press it open. Center the zipper, right side down, over the seam allowance, and baste. Using a zipper foot, topstitch $^3/_8$" from each side of the seamline, sewing across the tape at the closed end of the zipper. ▽

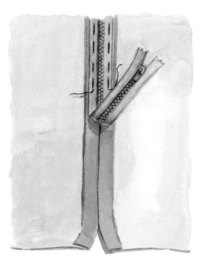

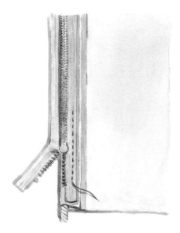

Piped or Welted Zipper

Install on a piped seam, as on the side back vertical edge of a slipcover. The welting masks the zipper. Sew the seam, leaving open the portion where the zipper will go. Press under the seam allowance in the open area. Open the zipper and position it so the welting just covers the zipper teeth. (Be sure the open end of the zipper is at the open end of the seam, if there is one.) With a zipper foot, stitch in the ditch of the welting seam through all layers. Close the zipper. Align the opposite (folded) edge of the open seam with the piping seamline, covering the zipper teeth; baste the zipper in place. Open the zipper and stitch $^1/_8$" from the teeth. △

Ties

To construct a simple narrow tie, cut a strip of fabric on the straight grain, making it four times the finished width of the tie and long enough to make one or more ties, including seam allowance in the length. Fold the strip in half lengthwise, right side out, and press. Open out the strip and then fold each long edge to the center creaseline, press. Fold the strip in half lengthwise and press again. Cut the strip into pieces of the appropriate length. Topstitch each tie closed, first turning in the seam allowance at one or both ends, as needed. (If one end of the tie will be inserted in a seam, leave the end unfinished.) ▽

Buttonholes

The size of a buttonhole should always be determined by the size of the button. Minimum buttonhole length should equal the diameter plus the thickness of the button, plus an additional $1/8$" to allow for the shank and a slight size reduction due to fabric thickness. Machine buttonholes should be made through at least two layers of fabric, and many times a piece of interfacing or a third layer of fabric should be added. Always test the buttonhole on a scrap of your fabric.

Buttons

To attach a sew-through button, wax a strand of thread, place it in a needle, and knot it. Insert the needle and thread from the wrong side of the fabric up through one hole in the button. Place a toothpick across the button between the holes. Take several stitches through the holes, making the stitches parallel to the corresponding buttonhole. Bring the needle and thread out between the button and fabric. Remove the toothpick, and lift button away from the fabric so the stitches are tight against button. Wind the thread around the stitches several times to form a shank. Secure the thread on the right side with several small stitches close to the shank. △

TIPS FROM THE PROS

✂When sewing buttons to thin or loosely woven fabric, reinforce the point of attachment by placing a small, flat button on the wrong side of the fabric. Stitch through both buttons and form a shank under the functional button as described above.

✂You can use a piece of interfacing in place of the second button. For sheers, use a piece of the same fabric.

SLIPCOVERING A SOFA BED

A slipcover for a sofa bed is essentially the same as one for a regular sofa. The only thing you must do differently is to leave the tuck-in around the seat unsewn. The seam between the seat front and the deck becomes a hinge. When you wish to pull out the mattress frame, fold the deck forward onto the floor.

There are a few things you can do to make a sofa bed slipcover longer wearing and easier to handle. Professionals usually pad the deck with thin foam and line it with denim or drill (another sturdy cotton twill fabric). This helps it to lie flat when the sofa is closed and topped with cushions. If you wish, you can add ties or straps to the side back edge of the deck and fasten them around the pull-out frame. You'll have to undo them to open the mattress, but they can be refastened around the open frame, thus lifting the deck off the floor.

TIPS FROM THE PROS

✂If you wish, you can make the deck of any slipcover from an inexpensive fabric. Topstitch a band of the outer fabric along the front of the deck before sewing the deck to the seat front. Should the deck slide forward under the cushions, the inexpensive fabric will not show.

essential equipment

Probably the most important aid you need for slipcover making, aside from a reasonably sturdy sewing machine, is a well-lit workspace—of course the larger, the better. There are many tools and materials that smooth the slipcovering process. While some of these are common household items, you'll find that items designed for specific tasks save time and give professional results. Most of these are available at fabric, art supply, or home stores. If you have trouble locating something, refer to the ads in a sewing magazine for a mail-order vendor.

FOR MEASURING AND MARKING

Measuring and marking aids are used when you are planning your slipcover, making patterns, and marking cutting and seam lines. Having a variety of these items ensures accuracy and saves time.

Tape Measure
A flexible cloth or fiberglass tape, $1/2$" x 60", is essential for taking measurements around pieces of furniture. Look for one that is marked on both sides, with the numeral 1 at opposite ends.

Yardsticks and Rulers
Use to measure fabric width and yardage and to take straight, rigid furniture measurements, such as skirt height from floor to seamline. Use also as a measuring guide and straightedge when marking bias strips and other cutting lines on fabric.
✄Wooden yardsticks (1" x 36") are readily available; check for warping if using as a straightedge.

✄Rulers can vary in length from 6" to 30" and can be made of wood or metal; they also come in clear, grid-printed plastic, which is handy when ruling on seam allowance.
✄Larger metal rulers are available; 2" x 48" is a handy size for marking out large pieces.

T-Square and L-Square
Useful for measuring 45- and 90-degree angles and for finding and marking the lengthwise, crosswise, or bias grain on fabric. Can be made of metal or plastic.

45-degree Right-Angle Triangles
Made of clear plastic and available in many sizes, these are especially useful for finding and marking fabric bias.

TIPS FROM THE PROS
✄Purchase metal rulers, squares, and triangles at fabric, quilting, or art supply stores, where they are available in lightweight aluminum that slides easily over fabric on the cutting table. The carpenter's rulers available in home and hardware stores are too heavy.

French Curves
Plastic templates with variously curved perimeters. Use to smoothly mark any curved edge, especially on rounded corners or scroll-shaped pieces. The curves are fairly small; slide and rotate them as needed to establish clean lines.

Seam Gauge
Small metal ruler with a sliding marker. Great for marking seam and hem lines and for checking smaller measurements during construction.

Pencil
Use to mark clear, long-lasting cutting and seam lines and match marks. If the fabric will be laundered, a regular lead pencil makes a good marker. Erasable pencil markers in a variety of colors are available in fabric stores.

TIPS FROM THE PROS
✄Keep an electric pencil sharpener nearby—you're likely to be marking a lot of long lines.

Dressmaker's Chalk
Use to make temporary marks (seamlines, pleats, ease areas, etc.) on fabrics. Since dressmaker's chalk can be brushed off after use, marks can be made on the right side of the fabric.
✄Available in block or pencil form, chalks come in a variety of colors.
✄Also available is a refillable powdered chalk dispenser with a wheel marker that makes crisp lines—it's great used along a ruler.

Transfer Paper and Tracing Wheels
These are found in all fabric stores. Use them to quickly transfer seamlines and match marks to multiple pieces. One side of the paper is coated with a waxy transfer medium. A path traced by a wheel run over the wrong side of the paper will transfer marks to whatever faces the right side, so place the paper between pattern and fabric, or between layers of fabric, as needed.
✄The paper comes packaged in a mix of colors; some notions stores carry large (2' x 3') sheets. Not all transfer paper marks wash out, so test on a scrap, try to use on the wrong side of the fabric, and be very careful using on sheers.

✂Tracing wheels come with smooth, serrated, or needlepoint edges. The smooth edge leaves a solid line; the serrated, a closely spaced dotted line. The needlepoint leaves a more widely spaced dotted line and, though it may mar sheers, it is useful for marking heavier fabrics.

TIPS FROM THE PROS

✂Use a needlepoint tracing wheel to transfer marks from a mock-up to a paper pattern or to complete a paper half-pattern. The spiky wheel leaves a perforated line in the paper, so no transfer paper is necessary; you can true up the marks with pencil and ruler.

Nonpermanent Ink Markers

A felt-tip marking pen that has either evaporating or water-soluble ink. The evaporating variety can be used on either the wrong or right side of the fabric; it evaporates in less than forty-eight hours. Water-soluble ink disappears when treated with water; test on a swatch for complete removal before using on the right side of fabric.

Quilter's Masking Tape

A narrow tape used as a seam allowance guide or to hold two pieces of fabric together until they can be sewn. The tape is easily removable and leaves no residue unless left on the fabric for more than eight hours.

Twill Tape

Inexpensive, flat cotton tape with a close herringbone weave. It is readily available in many widths. Use to establish and mark seamlines on the furniture itself before measuring.

FOR CUTTING

Cutting blades should be strong and sharp and should never be used to cut anything but fabric and thread. Maintain your cutting blades by having them regularly ground/sharpened by a professional.

Shears

Handles curved or bent at an angle allow shears to lie flat and glide on the cutting surface while cutting the fabric. Use heavy-duty shears with long (8") blades to cut decorator and upholstery fabrics. Use smaller shears with 6" or 7" blades to trim and grade seams. Use inexpensive shears to cut paper.

Sewing Scissors

Handles are straight rather than angled, so do not glide along the cutting table. Use scissors with small short blades for clipping and trimming seams, and for trimming threads.

Pinking Shears

Heavy-bladed shears with a serrated edge that are useful for trimming the raw edges of ravel-prone fabrics.

TIPS FROM THE PROS

✂Keep pinking shears away from pins when cutting. Once pinking shears are damaged, it is very difficult to have them properly sharpened.

Seam Ripper

To avoid snipping your fabirc, use this handy device instead of scissors to rip out incorrect seams. Slip the point under a single stitch and slide the blade to cut the thread.

Weights

Use to hold paper or muslin pattern pieces in place on the fabric while you are cutting. Made of metal, and often shaped like flat discs with a hole in the center, they can be purchased in fabric and craft stores.

Rotary Cutter, Cutting Mat, and Heavy Plastic Rulers

This cutting system is used extensively by quilters and makes short work of cutting multiple straight pieces, such as bias strips and ties. However, the size of your cutting mat determines the longest cut you can make, so the rotary cutting system may be cumbersome for large slipcover pieces.

✂The rotary cutter looks a lot like a pizza cutter. It has a circular blade that snaps in and out of a plastic handle; the blade can be smooth-edged or pinked-edged. Rotary cutters can give nasty cuts, so buy one with a retractable blade or protective shield, and keep away from children.

✂Cutting mats are made of a special plastic that is self-healing. They come in many sizes and colors, but all have 1" grids printed on the surface as guides for straight line cutting. Some mats have printed diagonal lines in addition to the grid.

✂Heavy transparent gridded rulers serve as measuring and cutting guides.

Rotary cutting is unlike cutting with shears because you always cut pieces from the left- rather than the right-hand edge of your fabric. If you are new to rotary cutting, make a few sample cuts to see how it works. (If you are left-handed, reverse the following directions.)

Using the Rotary Cutter

1 First mark a straight edge on your fabric. Place the mat on your table, then place the fabric, marked side up, on the mat. Place the ruler on your fabric, aligned with and to the left of your marked line. Hold the ruler firmly in place with your left hand; hold the cutter with your right hand. Place the blade against the edge of the ruler and apply pressure as you roll the blade away from you to cut along the marked line. Lift the ruler and discard the excess fabric.

2 Once you have cut a straight edge, you won't have to mark any other cutting lines. Align the cut edge of the fabric with a straight line on the cutting mat; the fabric should extend to your right. Align the appropriate guideline on the ruler with the cut edge of the fabric. (For instance, to cut a 2"-wide strip, align the line 2" from the edge of the ruler with the cut edge of the fabric—a 2" width of the ruler should overlap the fabric.) Cut along the edge of the ruler as you did in step 1. Lift the ruler, remove the cut width of fabric, and repeat as necessary. ▽

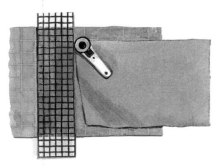

FOR FITTING AND SEWING

You won't need any unusual equipment for fitting and sewing most slipcovers, but the heavier your fabric, the sturdier your machine, thread, and pins should be. If your project is large, be sure your machine is in or on as big a table as possible—this will keep the weight of your project from pulling on the needle, which produces poor seams, or from sliding onto the floor, where it might be soiled.

Pins

While you can use standard dressmaker's (stainless steel) pins for home decorating projects, the following are often better alternatives when working with bulkier and heavier decorator fabrics:

✄Quilting Pins: 1¹/₄" long with large round heads at the top, they look like long dressmaker's pins.

✄T-Pins: Longer yet than quilting pins, the blunt end of this pin is folded perpendicular to the shaft, making a T shape. Useful when working with bulky and heavy fabrics, and for anchoring fabric to a padded surface.

✄Glass Head Pins: Fine and super sharp pins with small glass heads (won't melt with heat while pressing) for sheer and lightweight fabrics.

Adhesives, Interfacings, and Stabilizers

There are a number of products available that help to control fabric, give it body, or hold it together. Some are used to speed or ease the sewing process, while others give permanent support.

✄Interfacings: These woven or nonwoven fabrics are used to reinforce stress points and lend support to fragile fabrics. They are fused or basted to the fabric and the two layers are then treated as one. Back button and buttonhole areas with interfacing; place it in facings if your fabric is soft or sheer. If you are not familiar with the various types, ask your fabric vendor for assistance.

✄Fusible Webs: These look like lightweight nonwoven interfacing, but they are really sheets of glue. Place them between two pieces of fabric and press to adhere. They tend to add stiffness, but can be useful for small areas. Some webs come in strips that are suitable for hems. Fusible webs are generally permanent.

✄Sprays: There are permanent and temporary spray adhesives available in both art supply and sewing stores. They are particularly useful if you are layering batting with another fabric, as they save a lot of pinning and ensure a smooth surface. Spray them lightly onto the back of one fabric and then adhere it to another. Test the various products (follow the manufacturer's instructions) to be sure you like the way they work on your fabric.

✄Stabilizers: There is a whole world of temporary stabilizers, which are used to lend body to fabric during embroidery or quilting, thus preventing puckering. They either wash off, tear away, or brush off.

Threads

Pick the thread that matches the job. When in doubt about color, choose a shade that is slightly darker than the background of your fabric.

✂All-Purpose Thread: 100% polyester or cotton-covered polyester, this thread is suitable for most projects.

✂Hand-Basting Thread: Loosely twisted white (only) cotton thread for hand basting fabric pieces; breaks easily.

✂Upholstery Thread: 100% nylon or 100% polyester, extra strong for sewing heavyweight fabrics. Since it's treated to resist chemicals, rot, and mildew, it's an excellent choice for outdoor items.

✂Woolly Nylon Thread: Texturized overlock thread that is soft and strong, with ability to stretch and recover. Used primarily for serger rolled hems.

✂Button, Carpet, Heavy-Duty, and Craft Threads: Strong, heavy, cotton-covered polyester, designed specifically for hand sewing. Use to attach buttons to pillows and cushions.

Beeswax

To keep your thread from tangling or knotting when you are sewing by hand, pass it over the surface of a cake of beeswax. Also controls static electricity in synthetic threads.

TIPS FROM THE PROS

✂To augment the effect of beeswax, press the strand of waxed thread with a hot iron.

Sewing Machine

Every part of a home decorating project can be sewn on any standard, modern home sewing machine, even the hem. Be sure to use the proper needle size and type for your fabric—consult your owner's manual if unsure.

Serger

A great time saver that simultaneously stitches, trims, and overcasts a seam, performing all three operations at one time at twice the speed of a conventional home sewing machine. If you are not familiar with sergers, test one before purchasing—and be aware that pins must be removed from seams before reaching the needle and knife. Sergers can also create a narrow, rolled hem, and an edge finish that consists of small, tight stitches and no visible hem allowance, like those on commercially made napkins.

Embroidery Machine

Embroidery machines have the ability to stitch larger motifs, such as monograms and multicolored patterns, in unlimited varieties. Use to create a custom, decorative trim wherever you wish. Some machines can be attached to a PC and scanner to customize designs. Some manufacturers supply sewing machines that have built-in embroidery mechanisms, while others have a separate embroidery unit. Many modern home sewing machines are equipped with some embroidery stitches.

Sewing Machine Feet

Aside from a zipper foot, your regular straight sewing foot is all you really need for any home decorating project. However, some of the following special feet can make certain jobs easier. If you are unfamiliar with them, refer to your owner's manual.

✂Gathering Foot: Draws up the fabric to lock fullness into each stitch. Great for gathering long ruffles or lace trims evenly.

✂Ruffler Attachment: A large accessory designed to ruffle the edge of fabric in even spacings. The density of the gathering can be adjusted.

✂Hemming Foot: Automatically rolls the fabric into a narrow hem. Usually available in at least two widths. Hemming feet can be tricky to use, especially on bias edges, so test on a swatch of your fabric.

TIPS FROM THE PROS

✂If you have trouble getting good results with a hemming foot when your machine is set to straight stitch, try it with a zigzag stitch. Be sure the resulting effect is right for your project before using.

✂Quilting Foot: Has short, open toes to help you see and stitch along any lines or markings on the fabric.

✂Zipper Foot: A narrow presser foot that sits on one side of the needle only. Essential for inserting zippers and for covering and applying welting. If you are using welting, you'll need an adjustable zipper foot—one that can be positioned on either side of the needle—or a pair of fixed feet.

✂Piping Foot: A presser foot with a cut-out groove on the underside that guides cording evenly and consistently past the needle.

✂Edgestitch Foot: The upright flange of this foot rides along the edge of a fold or seamline, acting as a guide for straight edgestitching. Adjust the machine needle to the desired distance from the edge and sew, guiding the edge under the flange.

✂Blind Hem Foot: Designed for use with a zigzag stitch, this foot guides the fabric and enables you to quickly produce a nearly invisible hem.

essential equipment

✂Foot-Lifter for Bulky Intersections: This small device is not a foot, but enables your presser foot to ride over bulky intersecting seams without skipping stitches or chewing up the fabric. Slip it under the foot as needed and remove when you've stitched across the seam.

FOR PRESSING

All you really need for pressing a slipcover project is a decent iron and a sturdy ironing board. However, there are many other pressing aids; the various blocks and small boards not only help with specific pressing tasks, they enable you to press just a small area while the bulk of your project is supported by your ironing board—rather than dragging on the floor.

Iron

A standard steam/dry iron is fine for all projects. If using the steam setting, be sure your iron does not spit, and fill it with distilled water as a precaution against stains. Use with a press cloth or press on the wrong side of the fabric.

Steam Press

A commercial-type press now made in various models for the home sewer, it presses large areas efficiently. Also good for fusing large amounts of fusible interfacings.

Pressing Cloth

Use between the iron and fabric to prevent scorch and shine. Commercial versions are available in fabric stores, but a piece of muslin, batiste, or a tea towel (not terry cloth) works too.

Padded Surface

Press seams, tucks, pleats, darts, hems, etc., on a flat, stable, padded surface, such as an ironing board or a table or surface that is protected with a thick felt pad, wool blanket, cotton batting, or commercially prepared ironing board pad.

TIPS FROM THE PROS

✂Cover the padded pressing surface with heavy cotton fabric, such as drill—Teflon-treated covers are nonabsorbent and repel steam, so the fabric being pressed on them tends to lift or shift position.

Seam Roll

Press long seams, zipper applications, and narrow areas over this densely stuffed, fabric-covered roll, which is about 2" in diameter.

Hams

Mold and shape darts, curved and shaped seams, and hard-to-reach places by pressing them over a ham. Available in several shapes and sizes, these fabric-covered forms are either filled with finely processed sawdust or are molded in polyurethane.

Clapper

To flatten bulky seams, facings, creases, pleats, and points, place them on the pressing surface and pound gently with a clapper. Made of a smooth high-quality hardwood.

Point Presser

Slide the pointed end of this narrow, shaped hardwood block inside corners, points, and other hard-to-reach places.

Sleeve Board

A double-sided small ironing board for narrow, hard-to-reach places. Most sleeve boards collapse for storage.

Pile-Surfaced Boards

To avoid crushing pile or napped fabrics, press them face down on one of several types of pile-surfaced boards. The most traditional is a needle board, which is a specially constructed bed of steel needles set upright in a fabric pad. There are newer varieties, one of which resembles a field of hook-and-loop fastener hooks. If you are making a velveteen slipcover, buy the largest board you can afford so that you can press the largest possible area at one time.

TIPS FROM THE PROS

✂When using a needle board, avoid pressing along the edge of the needle bed—it will leave a permanent mark on most pile fabrics.

Bias Binding Maker

When strips of bias fabric are fed through this handy device they emerge with both long edges folded to the center, so they are easy to press into binding. Bias binding makers are available in sizes that produce $1/2$"-, $3/4$"-, 1"-, and 2"-wide folded tapes.

index

Page numbers in **bold** refer to Designer Details; those in *italic* indicate a photograph.

adhesives, 124
allowances, adding, 102
apron, for chair, 85–87, *85, 86*

basting, 114
batting, 117
bench, slipcover for, 69–73, *69, 71, 73*
bias, bias binding, *33, 51, 53,* 118–19
    cutting strips, 108
    decorative, *33,* **35**
    French fold, 40, 108, 118
    joining strips, 117
    mitering corners of, **52–53**
borders
    contrasting, *37, 38,* **38,** *67*
    scalloped-edged, *69, 71, 73* **73**
bows, *33, 34, 35, 40, 44, 48, 49, 51, 53, 54, 55,* 62–64, *63, 65, 85, 86,* 104
    decorative, **65**
boxing, 101
button(s), 121
    decorative, *27, 37, 38*
    tabs for, 74–78, *75, 76,* **79**
    loops for, 82–84, *84*
buttonholes, 121

cable cord, 119
chairs, slipcovers to make for, 33–34, *33, 34,* 36–38, *37, 38,* 39–41, *39, 40,* 42–44, *43,* 45–46, *45, 46,* 50–51, *50, 51,* 62–64, *63, 64,* 66–68, *67,* 74–78, *75, 76,* 82–84, *83, 84,* 93–94, *93, 95*
closures, 14. *See also* bows, button, ties
cording, *12, 22, 56, 57, 75, 76, 81, 89, 93, 95,*
    covered, *40,* **41,** 83
    joining twisted, 119

corners, sewing, 116
couches, slipcovers to make for, 48–49, *48, 49. See also* sofas
couching, *32,* **32**
curves, sewing, 116
cutting, 106–8
    tools for, 123–24

dart miters, 112
darts, *48, 49,* 111
daybed, slipcover for, 54–55, *55*
drawing, schematic, 103

edges, edging
    binding, *33, 34, 35,* **35,** *51, 53,* **52–53**
    finishing, 114
    rickrack, *43, 44,* **44**
    scalloped, *69, 71, 73,* **73**
    welted, 39–41, *39, 40*
embellishments, 14, *23*
embroidery machine, 125
equipment, 122–26

fabric
    apparel, 18
    cost, 11, 21
    decorator, 18
    fiber content, 18–19
    measuring, 100
    motif, 105, 106–7
    napped, 99
    positioning, 109
    preshrinking, 106
    pressing, 106
    railroaded, 99, 104, 107
    repeat, 100, 105
    right side/wrong side, 107
    selecting, 16–21
    suitability of, 15, 17, 20
    texture of, 17
    vertically run, 99, 104, 107
    weave, 20

fastenings, 120–21
fitting, 110–13
    tools for, 124. *See also* pin fitting
fringe, *12,* 14, *22, 23,* 80–81, *81,* 119
futon, sham for, 30–32, *31*

gathered skirts, *63, 67, 81,* 120
gathers, 111, 114
grain, of fabric, 107

hems, 117
    allowances, 102
    contrasting band, *37,* 38, 66
    mitered, *45, 46, 47,* **47**
    rolled, 115
    sheer, *85, 86*
    stitch-turn-stitch, 115
hook-and-loop tape, 120

interfacings, 124

layout, graph paper, 104–5

marking, 107
    tools for, 122–23
measuring, 100–3
    tools for, 122–23. *See also* yardage
miters, mitering, 45, 46, 47, **47,** *51, 53,* **52–53**
motifs, placing, 106–7

ottomans, slipcovers for, 56–57, *57,* 80–81, *81*

patterns
    matching, 20, 105, 106
    paper, 104
pin fitting, 109–13
pins, 124
plaids, 20, *56–57*
pleats, *37, 59, 60, 83, 84, 85, 86, 93,* 103
    spaced boxed, *93,* **95**

index

acknowledgments

PHOTOGRAPHY ACKNOWLEDGMENTS
Part One
8–9: Ralph Bogertman; stylist: Susan Piatt; table: Pottery Barn. **10:** Richard Mandelkorn; designer: Celeste Cooper. **11:** Earl Carter/BELLE/ARCAID; designer: Christian Liaigre. **12–13:** Phillip Ennis; designer: Howard Slatkin. **14:** John M. Hall; designer: Frank Faulkner. **15:** Scott Francis/ESTO. **16–17:** Fred Lyon. **19:** John M. Hall. **20:** Dennis Krukowski; designer: Tunin MacCallum A.S.I.D., Inc. **21:** Dennis Krukowski; designer: Abby Darer Interior Design. **22:** Dennis Krukowski; designer: Tunin MacCallum A.S.I.D., Inc. **25:** John M. Hall; designer:

Sig Bergman. All fabric baskets and trimmed swatches: Ralph Bogertman.
Part Two
33, 34, 35: Philip Harvey. **26–27, 39, 40, 45, 46, 47, 89, 90, 91, 92, 93, 95:** Ralph Bogertman; stylist: Susan Piatt; table, page 39: Pottery Barn. **All other photographs:** Brian Kraus NYC; prop stylist: Rachel A. Tucker.
Part Three
96–97: Ralph Bogertman.

PROJECT ACKNOWLEDGMENTS
Slipcover samples were made by Linda Lee Design Associates, Topeka, Kansas, with help from Stephanie Valley, Darchelle

Woltkamp, Lane's Custom Interiors, Marge Cole, Dort Johnson, Bernie Holsteen, Pat Thomas, Russ' Custom Upholstery.

The editors would like to thank the following for assistance with materials for the samples. Covington Industries, Inc./Spectrum Fabrics generously donated the fabrics for the projects beginning on the following pages: 36, 39, 42, 45, 58, 62, 69, 82, 88, 93 (diamond fabric). Conso, Hollywood Trims, Streamline Buttons, and Threadwear donated buttons and trims. Thanks also to Kravet Fabrics, Inc., Westgate Fabrics, and Stroheim & Romann, Inc.